BOBBE
BAGGIO,
PH.D.

AI @ WORK

HOW ARTIFICIAL INTELLIGENCE IS CHANGING
THE WAY WE WORK

Copyright © 2022 Bobbe Baggio Ph.D.

All rights reserved. In accordance with the U.S. Copyright Act of 1976, the scanning, uploading, and electronic sharing of any part of this book without the permission of the publisher constitutes unlawful piracy and theft of the author's intellectual property. If you would like to use material from the book (other than for review purposes), prior written notice must be obtained by contacting the publisher at http: www.a-l-t.com or email permissions@a-l-t.com

Advantage Learning Press is a division of Advantage Learning Technologies, Inc. The logo is the trademark of Advantage Learning Technologies, Inc. All rights reserved.

First Edition: 2022

Library of Congress Control Number: 2022915871

ISBN: 978-0-9914051-7-6

Ebook and Print Interior Design by Steven W. Booth, www.GeniusBookServices.com

Cover Design by Senhor Tocas, www.SenhorTocasIllustrator.tumblr.com

Table of Contents

Fast Forward 1

Chapter 1: After Years of "AI's Coming," It's Finally Here. 5

Chapter 2: AI and the Agile Workplace 21

Chapter 3: Disruption and Obsolescence 41

Chapter 4: From Great to Gone 55

Chapter 5: Disappearing Jobs and the Future....................................71

Chapter 6: AI and Big Work-Life Changes 89

Chapter 7: Agile Transformation 107

Chapter 8: AI and Education Reborn 123

Chapter 9: Blockchain Edu... 141

Chapter 10: Robotic Process Automation 157

Chapter 11: Intangible Assets.. 175

Chapter 12: Uncoded Bias in AI 187

Chapter 13: Privacy and Ethics.. 201

Chapter 14: Working With Humans 221

References 237

Glossary of Acronyms..261

Index.. 265

About the Author...271

For K1, K2 and K3

Fast Forward

This book explores the impact of artificial intelligence on the workplace, human performance, and learning and development. AI is all around us. It has become an everyday thing. It helps us, it frustrates us and sometimes it makes us laugh. It impacts how we work, where we work and what we do at work. After years of "the robots are coming," the bots have arrived. It's hard these days to talk to a human in customer service. Barriers to entry kept AI at bay for decades, then it all changed. Google knew your birthday and Alexa and Siri were making recommendations for songs to listen to and recipes for dinner. AI and workplace disruption has only begun. Society hasn't really felt the impact of this technology yet. Not like it will in the next few decades. Disruption of this magnitude will shake up how we work, learn and play on every level. It's time to start thinking and planning for a new way of life. Let's not get caught in the same traps we did when the Internet opened up data, privacy and a hole other can of worms.

AI will be bigger, more impactful and disrupt our lives even more quickly than the Internet did. Terms like deep learning, machine learning, big data, and little data are part of everyday conversations. The engineering of AI has begun. Now is the time to ask questions. What do we want AI to do? How can it help people? How might it hurt people? How will it reframe business processes? AI took a long time coming but now that it is here, it demands our attention and respect. Because without our respect, humanity is in trouble. This technology is powerful. More powerful than any other we've ever known.

Most AI today is based on semantic language processing. Language translations and understanding has moved AI closer to providing humans with non-human conversant assistants. Slowly since the 1960s MIT, IBM, CMU (Carnegie Mellon University), Stanford and many other think tanks have moved AI forward. No one has contributed as much as DARPA (Defense Advanced Research Projects Agency). There are a lot of players in the AI arena now and many of them have a lot of skin in the game. Amazon, Meta, IBM, Google, Apple, Microsoft; the current tech giants are all in. There is not one definition of AI. Generally, AI describes machines doing work that would normally require humans to do it. From the beginning AI has been plagued with duality. The more pervasive the technology becomes the more we begin to start to understand the challenges of having machines that can "think."

With every new technology comes displacement and upheaval. The workplace is transformed and rearranged. AI is certainly no exception and has the potential to be the most disruptive yet. AI is both accessible and powerful. It has the potential to do a tremendous amount of good. It also has the potential to turn our world upside down, displacing millions in the workplace, eliminating jobs and creating incredible inequalities. It also has the potential for doing great good. AI is ready to solve problems, take over redundant and menial tasks and free up humans to live a life based of fulfilling the needs of people not just business. AI meets people where they are. Whether it is a robot on the assembly line or a chatbot on your phone or a website, AI goes to where people need it.

AI requires monitoring because it is moving so quickly. High quality and consistent data is a must with an emphasis on how this technology affects human beings. From HR to the production floor there is a great emphasis on AI to support rapid change. There also needs to be a transparency and auditing as AI evolves because the impact on our workplace will be huge. The workplace and the educational system have to keep pace in a world that is changing and adapting new technologies very quickly. We have entered the world of everyday AI.

New technologies always bring upheaval and displacement. The workplace is transformed and rearranged. AI is certainly no exception to the rule. Business and capitalism is driving and will continue to drive the deployment of AI but humans need to be the voice that contributes to how AI is used.

When business processes change, it requires education and support. Change is not easy for humans. We need to become experts in risk management, flexibility and change. All areas where humans don't usually excel. AI can also shine a light on areas of neglect within the company. Structures of organizations and internal systems that don't connect and don't communicate. Structures that require tedious and meaningless data entry and redundancy. Data is stored in silos: the financial systems, the HR systems, the customer support systems, etc. AI also has risk factors associated with its algorithms, programing and assumptions.

It's impossible to talk AI without talking about privacy. Very little has been put into place to assure data privacy and restrict public access or use. There is also the issue of bias. One study showed that Google recommended higher paying jobs to men more often than to women. It's time to consider regulatory and legal measures to assure that AI works for humans. This puts the spotlight on training and education. Companies and organizations need and will continue to need talent. The skills gap will increase as technologies continue to evolve. It is not just about new algorithms and systems; ultimately it's about people. The threat to jobs is only partly about automation. Big changes will impact skills and job rolls, and will support training and retraining workers.

The nature of work is changing, and it is changing rapidly. Never underestimate the importance of human creativity and mental flexibility. Learning needs to be ongoing and complete. Ultimately it's all about human talent. The future will require continued learning and relearning. Agile is about being awake, alert, vigilant and prepared. Agile is the key to our future. Get ready to learn!

AI is an everyday thing. The major AI systems are everywhere in our lives. Google says, "Happy Birthday"! Amazon's Alexa asks if there is anything else she can do after she turns off the lights. We pull into the drive-in window at McDonald's and the conversation is with "bots," (voice recognition technologies) not people. It's hard these days to talk with a human. AI is at work, online and even at the train station. Bots have taken over. The barriers to entry, that kept AI at bay for decades, has somehow slipped away. A wide range of products, services and applications emerged, right under our noses, and all are AI. AI has become part of our world. Society hasn't really felt the disruption yet. Not like we will in the next decades. Estimates of worker displacement range between 48% in the U.S. to 70% in India. Humans are not paying attention. AI is no longer a future technology. It is here now, and it is here to stay.

Chapter 1

After Years of "AI's Coming," It's Finally Here.

"People worry that computers will get too smart and take over the world, but the real problem is that they're too stupid and they've already taken over the world."
—Pedro Domingos

The focus is starting to shift toward impact. Terms like big data, little data, machine learning, and deep learning are all a part of our language. Scientists aren't just thinking about how AI works. Now it's about how it can work for people. Marty the robot at the local grocery store roams the aisles asking to help locate products. Voices pop up on your smartphone. AI is here. The engineering part is being conquered. Now it is a question of a shared vision. What do we want AI to do? Can it help people? Will it reframe business processes? Everyone, not just technical people, needs to play a role in these decisions. AI is here and ready to solve problems for everyone. It affects all aspects of our lives.

AI took a long time coming but now that it is here, AI demands respect. Researchers, engineers, designers, dialogue experts, voice talent, inclusion and diversity experts and many more talented people need to get involved. Otherwise, humanity is in big trouble. The results could be not only troubling but inhumane. AI is moving quickly, very quickly. It has taken on a life of its own. Anyone who is responsible for redundant and repetitive tasks is at risk of replacement. AI is about making decisions and judgments. Things that in the past were part of only the human domain. It is ripe with complexities, challenges, and potential. AI is taking on problems. It is discovering unrealized opportunities and identifying new actions. It can and will solve problems. It is finding its way into every nook and cranny of industry and every aspect of our lives.

AI has been on the horizon for decades. The challenges and fantasies surrounding AI include ideas from many disciplines. AI holds the promise of new possibilities. It offers infinite promise and a way of defining what it means to be human. In the mid-1940s, talks on the nature of intelligence laid the foundations for computer processing. Philosophers like Gottfried Wilhelm Leibniz and Blaise Pascal reflected on the design of intelligent machines. Jules Verne (Around the World in Eighty Days), Isaac Asimov (I, Robot), Frank Baum (The Wizard of Oz) and many others imagined smart machines. These machines were capable of interaction with human beings. They supported and challenged our deepest concerns on being human (Buchanan, 2006).

Both the fields of AI and Machine Learning (ML) have grown. This goes well beyond any of the individual contributors. Nobert Wiener did work on cybernetics. W. Ross Ashby, Warren McCulloch and Walter Pitts worked on neural networks. Communication theory, mathematics and statistics, logic and philosophy, and linguistics helped to develop AI. John Von Neumann's and Oskar Morgenstern's additions to game theory added to AI and ML (Machine Learning). A landmark paper in Mind in 1950, which led to the Turing Test, was a major turning point in AI's evolutionary journey. The term AI was established at the 1956 Dartmouth Conference on Artificial Intelligence. The AI discussion continues to unfold. When AI is described, at the core of intelligence is always the concept of continued learning.

Most AI today, like it was in the 1960s, is based on natural language processing. Language was always thought to be the cornerstone of AI. Language is important because of the computer's ability to store and retrieve huge amounts of verbal data. Slowly, understanding began to creep into the landscape. Language insight and translations have moved AI closer to providing humans with personal assistants. Knowledge-based systems have overtaken logic-based paradigms. Gradually, since the 1960s, MIT, IBM, CMU, Stanford and many other think tanks have helped move AI forward. Today, the AI community is thriving.

AI and intelligent human behavior are not clearly defined. Typically, AI describes the process of machines doing work that would require human intelligence. The term usually includes examining intellect, problem solving and creating computer systems that are intelligent. Sometimes, AI is either weak or strong. Weak AI is a computer mimicking cognitive processes and simulating intelligence. Strong AI implies computers are self-learning and intelligent. Computers can understand and adjust their own behaviors based on prior knowledge or data. Other ways of describing AI include narrow, broad and channel. Narrow AI is the ability of AI to handle one specific task. This task duplicates or replaces human intelligence. Diagnosing skin cancer is an example of narrow AI. Broad AI is capable of exhibiting intelligent behaviors across many processes or tasks. Someday, broad AI systems may even exhibit other aspects of human intelligence. Channel AI is even broader, more influencing and more expansive (Wisskirchen, 2017) (Growth Stage Podcast, 2018).

What AI Is, and Isn't

From its beginning AI has been plagued with duality. Success in AI means increased social responsibilities and educational challenges. The impact of AI is difficult for decision makers and the public to understand. Significant progress has been made. Different combinations of reasoning are just a few of the aspects of intelligence. This is necessary for successful AI systems. The duality between the role of humans and the role of machines is only beginning to play out. AI offers humans benefits. These include fewer boring workplaces, safer manufacturing, better travel, and increased security. These smarter decisions may help preserve our volatile habitat (Buchanan, 2006).

Since the beginning, AI has been concerned with creating intelligent machines. These machines formalize thinking in all areas of the human experience. AI has always been about making it easier to work with computers and being more helpful. The impact of AI has the potential to meet and/or exceed any prior technologies. Exploring psychology, reasoning, decision science and behavior puts AI in the position to solve intellectual problems. It can control robotic motions, interpret human language, learn new skills and acquire knowledge by continually analyzing data.

What is so disturbing is that AI has been coming for so long and suddenly it's everywhere. AI has become an everyday technology. It is the start of a new chapter in human history. A chapter that can and will have a greater impact than almost anyone can imagine. A wide range of services, products and sources have contributed to the emergence of AI. It is time for our focus to shift from the technical aspects of AI to the impact it will have on human lives. It is no longer about when AI will it happen or how the technology can work. Rather it is about what AI can do for us. How will AI impact us, both positively and negatively? We have entered the world of everyday AI.

With every technology comes displacement and upheaval. The workforce is transformed and rearranged. AI is certainly no exception. It has the potential to be the most disruptive yet. Business will drive the deployment of AI. Humans in every aspect of society need to be involved in the voice that contributes to how AI is used.

AI is both accessible and powerful. It has the potential to do a tremendous amount of good. It also has the potential to turn our world upside down, displacing millions in the workplace, eliminating jobs and creating voids as well as opportunities. AI is ready to solve problems and take over redundant and menial tasks. Are humans ready to adapt and relearn? To create a new kind of workplace? One that is not based on the old vision of transactions, widgets and repetition. One that works towards fulfilling the needs of the people, not just business. AI meets people where they are. Whether it is a chatbot on a website or an app, or a robot on the assembly line, AI goes to the need.

AI Changes Everything

AI requires monitoring because it is moving so quickly. Robots are displacing people in almost all areas of the workplace, it is just a question of who and how. This means looking clearly at the technology. High quality, reliable, consistent data analysis is a must for AI. The focus of the impact of AI needs to stay on the human experience. Humans are ultimately responsible for the decisions AI is making. Automating cognition, judgment and reason is not without challenges. AI has a role to play in almost every industry which means it is mainstream and can and will have a huge impact on our workplace. It's time to talk. It's time to get a plan in place. Humanity is moving forward, and very quickly with installed AI (Moore, 2019).

Uber disrupted the transportation business, Airbnb the hotel business and Amazon just about every business. The question becomes one of speed and adaption. This requires a fundamental shift in how people view work. From HR to the production floor there is a great emphasis on using AI to support rapid change. The disruption is rampant. Industries, sectors, products and positions are transforming before our eyes. Work is no longer about just hiring people and tracking hours worked. It is about productivity, and the ability to respond quickly to changes in market conditions, customer demands and technological innovations. What will be done by AI and what will require human intervention? Business will need to hire smarter and train better. It will be crucial for businesses to acquire and keep the best talent. The world of robots makes treating humans with respect imperative. Humans seek more from work than robots. They need connection, meaning, value, development and acceptance.

The workplace and the educational system have to keep up with the rest of the world. Advances in technologies have made the world more accessible, convenient and enjoyable. AI, chatbots, vocally activated technology, machine learning, social platforms, mobile apps, virtual reality, mixed reality, adaptive technologies and a host of other technologies have found their way into our workplaces (Farrow, 2019).

AI offers tremendous potential. It can improve production and monitoring. It can improve quality control checks and regulating power. It can make production more efficient, and less dependent on humans. Flexible production is a biproduct of AI. Data analysis is everywhere. This brings prices down and increases quality. Using data in real time to adjust and create flexible processes has enormous potential. Modern manufacturing uses AI to customize products and for small production runs. AI is used for production robots and automated virtual assistants.

Price Waterhouse Cooper (PWC) suggests nearly 62% of large companies use AI. Quality control, testing and machine maintenance are only a few applications. Many solutions are going to the cloud. Data is collected worldwide. Data links processes, products, plants, machines and systems. It is all about optimizing production and making smarter decisions. Production becomes more reliable, products more dependable and companies more efficient.

All of this has happened very quickly. Although we have been testing AI for decades, AI only recently reached a tipping point. This puts a tremendous strain on the IT teams and raises big... or rather huge questions about risk, security and safeguards.

Better, Faster, Cheaper

Cybercrime is becoming more sophisticated and widespread. Everyone is scrambling for new security measures and better execution.

The level of support for the adoption of AI is basic economics. Better, faster, cheaper is the promise of AI. It will take talent and planning to make it happen. The more AI cloud-based applications, the less it costs to get into the game. Companies are determined to reap the benefits of AI. It is a balancing act between creating new cognitive technologies and the effective execution of these technologies. It is important they benefit everyone, not just a few. There is no shortage of enthusiasm or investment. Effective execution might be another story.

More companies are turning to vendors for cloud-based solutions. Everyone is getting in the game. It is all about competition. AI is a competitive advantage and is critical to strategic position. Systems with huge cloud-based data sets like CRM (Customer Relationship Management) and ERP (Enterprise Resource Planning) systems open the doors for using AI. CRM is software that lets the company track every transaction with clients and customers. ERP refers to software that helps manage processes that are going on across the enterprise.

AI and increased threat go hand in hand. This is because everything is digital. Companies are finding it easier and easier to use AI. More and more vendors are getting on the bandwagon. Modifying and customizing off-the-shelf applications is replacing the build-from-scratch approach. The cost and initial risk is coming down. Finally, the expectations for transformation are slowing a bit. This is because we are recognizing the complexities of installed AI. AI impacts the infrastructure and training and education. How we use AI and how we protect ourselves while using AI is a balancing act. One that society has not quite mastered. The promise of better, faster, cheaper products and processes and better decisions is offset by the realities and dangers of digitization.

Humans always complicate things. There is undoubtedly huge potential that will help humans and make the healthcare industry more efficient and cost effective. Once people get involved, using AI successfully can be more challenging. Healthcare is probably the most visible industry with high AI potential but low impact so far. Using AI for radiology and claims management has been a success, showing us again that redundant processes, either cognitive or task oriented, will be replaced.

Using AI requires companies to become experts at risk management, flexibility and change. Most companies are not good at this. In other words, agile. Many companies have seen AI projects fail. They fail not because the technologies are inferior. They fail because the humans who use the technologies are not ready to accept new ways of doing things. When humans don't understand and don't trust technologies the results can be less than ideal. Change is not easy and not something that humans embrace. When business processes change, every aspect should be examined. There are very few cases where robots are totally replacing humans. More commonly, AI is enhancing the business process. Hopefully, AI is making it more efficient, effective and flexible. In most cases humans are not eliminated but rather supported. Any kind of change, though, takes education and support.

AI also shines a spotlight on areas of neglect within a company. The internal systems that lack are not connected. They also have a large amount of redundancy. AI is all about the data and the data must have integrity. Customer data is in one system. The financial data in another system. The HR data in another and on and on.... These systems have never been integrated. AI requires data early and lots of it. Many companies find it too difficult and costly to mine the data. Often the data comes from multiple systems. Plus, companies must still protect privacy, security and make sure the data is reliable.

AI and Risk

There is no question that installed AI has a set of risk factors all its own. Fears of disruption, threats of infiltration and security risks cloud the safety and dependability of AI systems. System failures can add to the complexity of AI operations. Data can be lost. Deep learning uses data in image and speech recognition. The data involved and how it is used is really not understood by most humans.

The arrival of AI on a much larger scale has also opened questions of privacy. Although the robots are here, very little has been put into place as far as legal and regulatory preparations. Europe currently has the General Data Protection Regulation (GDPR). The U.S., China, India and other countries don't have much data protection. There is no question that cloud-based data has changed the way we connect the world. Life on the cloud for data has gained in popularity. Many companies and organizations are concerned, however, about risks vs. benefits.

Explaining how computers behave can be complex. It is a difficult endeavor even if people are willing to do it. Regulators are challenged by deep learning. They tend to look at AI models like black holes. The results can be accurate but "how we got there" remains a mystery. Companies are pouring huge amounts of money into explain-ability. We have had Facebook disasters and fake news in the 2016 U.S. elections. Everyone realizes there is an issue with false information and AI. Misuse of personal data can affect important life decisions. It affects credit worthiness, crime detection and bias. Biased data can generate biased results.

One study showed that Google showed ads for high paying jobs more to men than to women. These kinds of issues have challenged us to dig deep and consider what regulatory and legal measures are needed. We need regulation so that with AI we don't run the risk of discriminatory and offensive results. The arrival of AI is not without challenges.

Success moving forward depends on more than technology. The robots are here and now it is our job to make the robots (AI) work for humans. This puts a spotlight on training and education. Companies and organizations need and will continue to need talent. The skills gap will continue to increase because technologies will continue to evolve in complexity and scale. It is not just about new algorithms and systems. It's ultimately about people. There is an ongoing need to train AI experts.

We are obviously still trying to understand the huge changes facing the workforce. These changes will determine how and when training can be used to refocus and reposition humans. The magnitude of job loss in the coming decade will be extensive. The effect will reach far and deep. There are ethical consequences to these cuts in the workforce. We have only begun to feel the impact. To use a well-worn analogy, implementation of AI will be like a snowball rolling down a hill. AI presents the chance of blending the best of what machines can do with the best of what humans can do. Humans bring experience, judgment and empathy that coupled with AI augmentation will usher in new ways of working.

The threat to jobs is only partly about automation. Changes in the workplace will impact job rolls, skills, retraining and retaining workers. Companies and workers alike cannot be complacent. The AI revolution will affect all of us. Whether companies choose to hire from outside or retrain and reposition, continuing education and learning will play a huge role in our future. Ultimately, it is all about human talent.

AI and Power

AI can make workers better at their jobs. It can make them happier in their positions and more comfortable at home. It can empower people to make better decisions and increase job satisfaction. Both companies and individuals need sound strategies for talent development and continuing education. It's very important that we start now. The "arms race" for high quality technical talent has only begun. Technical talent is not the only talent that is needed for success. Companies need leadership. They need executives who can speak and understand the technologies. They need workers who understand the limitations and uses of data and analytics.

AI will help with automation and cut costs, but this is not the purpose of cognitive technology. In many situations, AI is simply better and more efficient than humans at performing a job. In these cases, jobs will be replaced. AI will stand alongside people helping to make predictions, offering alternatives and interpreting information. Automation and augmentation will work hand in hand as we move forward to the agile workplace.

As you read this book there are a few things to remember. The nature of work is changing, and it is changing rapidly. Technological advancements in cognitive technologies, robotics, AI, machine learning and deep learning are with us and will impact all our lives. Our challenge is to embrace the changes and make them work in our favor. There is no going backwards. Technology never goes back. Much of the work that humans do today will be automated in the next decade. Many new jobs will open up and many new roles will need training and education. Get ready to learn and to continue to learn is the message of the future workplace. Machines and humans are already engaged in a collaborative workplace and more so every day. The future is robo-human. The robots are already here. Now is the time to embrace change and figure out how education, governments and companies can prepare humans to be an active and productive part of it. Both technical skills and human skills will be needed in the workplace of the future. It's all about integration, augmentation and automation working hand in hand to provide humans with a better tomorrow.

Never underestimate the importance of human creativity and mental flexibility. Both will play a significant role in the workplace of tomorrow. We need to start to embrace change and teach these skills in the workplace and in schools. Not just give them lip service, but incorporate affective intelligence, logic, ethics, values and judgment into all curriculums. Most educational institutions and organizations including the governments of the world are not adapting quickly enough to the changes that are being initiated now let alone those that lie ahead.

According to Robot Ready, "The future of work is now and standing still is not an option. In order to shape the work of the future, organizations have a tremendous opportunity to redesign and cultivate this mindset of 'both, and' earlier in the learning process" (Robot Ready, 2019). Learning needs to be ongoing and complete. It needs to encompass those skills needed in the workplace and those skills that support the continuing evolution of humans. Humans need to learn and continue to learn both technical skills and human skills. This learning will take place in the classroom, on the job, in training, online and in all other environments humans inhabit.

Get ready to learn. The future is not one of stagnation but of continued growth. This growth will require the ability to integrate technical and human skills. We will continue to discover what businesses, organizations and humans need in the workplace. New skills will have to be learned and relearned. More new skills will be added to the inventory of both traditional education and workforce training. The skills gap needs to address people looking for good work. It needs to include companies looking for talent, educators and learning and development specialists.

Agile is the key to our future. How we get there is through continued improvement in AI and continued human learning. Agile is about being awake, alert, vigilant and prepared. Continuing change and growth are the foundations of an agile workplace. The agile workplace will require radical change by institutions and organizations. Changes in the way we do things and the mindset we bring to the tasks. Humans can look forward to a future where AI will bring vast improvements. There will be improvements in productivity, freedom from boring work and in quality of life.

ASK THE HARD QUESTIONS

- How will we use AI? How will we keep it from being abused?
- How will we measure success?
- How will we guard against disaster?
- How will AI affect the workplace? Your job? Future Jobs?

Chapter 2

AI and the Agile Workplace

"Failure is not fatal, but failure to change might be."
—John Wooden

There is no question that dramatic change is coming. The idea that entire occupations will be replaced by AI is probably overstated. Certain activities within occupations may be automated. As a result, the entire business process will be transformed. In the United States this translates to about two trillion dollars in annual wages. Professionals are not immune. Physicians, financial managers, CFOs, CEOs and senior executives will all have parts of their jobs automated. Research suggests automation will impact nearly 45% of the workplace. That is nearly one out of every two workers (Chui et al., 2015, p. 2).

Companies will be leaner and have less hierarchy. Every person between decisions and decision makers costs money. The impact on work will depend on if what you do is routine. It won't matter if it is cognitive or physical tasks. Routines are what AI does best (Wisskirchen et al., 2017, p. 48). Companies will focus on core competencies. They will outsource other areas of work. Data analysis will continue to be strongly fueled by "Big Data" and data science. More traditional specialists and support personnel may be outsourced. Companies will focus on professional connections. They will create a support structure outside the company. These experts will be the basis of success in the digital workplace.

The IOT (Internet of Things) will offer direct connections between customer and suppliers. There will be more autonomy for the worker. This will require more training and ongoing skill development. Matrix structures are already here. More companies may be using them to support both technical and human employment. One of the big questions is the sharing of economic risk. How will that be divided between employee and employer? The "Gig" Economy offers freedom and autonomy. The work on demand culture shares risks differently. Entrepreneurial risk has shifted with the independent contractor. This has advantages and drawbacks for both parties (Wisskirchen, et al., 2017).

The implication for employment dynamics and leadership is enormous. Leadership will need to align and redefine positions. Workplace performance will include the potential to automate and the economics of automation. The benefits can be much greater than the costs. The extent of automation suggests that the ability to lead and manage it will be a competitive difference. AI will support the automation and force companies to redefine jobs and business processes. In most cases, automation will meet or exceed the current level of humans on the job. AI will impact jobs. Retail sales, food and beverage servers, teachers and healthcare specialists are and will be affected. Less than 5% of all occupations will be fully automated but the impact on business and the workplace will be huge (Michael Chui et al., 2015, p. 5).

The Agile Workplace

The agile workplace offers workers a greater amount of meaningful work. AI will replace routine and repetitive services. Employees will be able to focus on creativity and human emotions. In the new workplace the focus will be on activities rather than occupations. As AI continues to unfold, it is important to develop agile work environments. Agile supports evolving business processes. Companies will become more service oriented. They will replace fixed operations with intelligent solutions. Fixed operations are replaced based on costs and benefits and business needs (Mircea, 2011).

Companies will leverage internal innovation, and their ecosystem of vendors and distributors. The organization's structure from the past will fade away. We are already using customer feedback in the form of surveys. Surveys gather the results of a process. These include product sales, customer experience, and enjoyable interactions. With AI, we can make rapid process changes. These will directly affect the successful outcome of a business. Enterprises will focus on a series of subsequent outcomes. These will lead to a business objective, regardless of who or where they are being performed.

The shift in focus will be toward work of higher value. Even the highest paid occupations will be supplemented by AI. Occupations like lawyers, professors, physicians, sales and many others will be enhanced. AI will be used for text mining and lead generation. This will leave the professionals to assume higher cognitive roles. These shifts will not be without challenges. Professionals will have time to practice soft skills, from running meetings to coaching, to interviewing and providing feedback. This will happen in a safe environment with the intent of teaching human to human interactions.

AI skills will expand and include diagnosis if you are a doctor, and selling skills if you are a salesperson. The workplace will be influenced by the coming together of multiple technologies. This will not be about one single technology. It will advance when business needs line up with high-tech options. Talent development will have the chance to create new processes, applications and solutions. New technologies will change the roles and interactions of employees (Wisskirchen et al., 2017). Workplace trends to watch are using AI for the intersection between business needs and redundant skills and services.

An agile workplace is one that moves quickly and easily. It adapts to varying situations and is perceptive and fluid. It is a workplace that adapts easily to changes. Everything is different every day and that's the way it flows. It welcomes change. It supports collaboration and interaction. It is built around motivated and intelligent humans who should and can be trusted. It adapts to regularly changing circumstances. The ability to automate job tasks has little to do with high wage vs. low wage occupations. It has more to do with redundancy and change. Some jobs like home healthcare workers, landscapers, maintenance workers, and social workers are safer. Any occupations that deal with an environment of constant change and challenge are less likely to be affected. The ability to create and interact with human emotion is difficult to automate. Only 4% of activities in the U.S. economy require creativity and spontaneity. Only 29% of activities require sensing human emotion (Chui et al, 2015). Both blue collar and white-collar workers will be affected. The faster the process steps can be described in detail and are shown to be repetitive, the sooner the employee can be replaced with AI (Wisskirchen et al., 2017).

Agility in the workplace means both flexibility and configurability. Flexibility is the organization's ability to adjust to the customers' needs. Configurability is the ability to adjust to changing demands. Agile work environments can and usually do support multiple intelligent agents in the supply chain. These agents are involved in one or more activities, and are flexible enough to adjust and reconfigure based on changing circumstances (Lou, et al., 2004).

In the beginning, agile applied to manufacturing environments. Now it encompasses all types of workplaces. It describes the company in terms of the collection of business processes. This time ordered sets of activities or tasks are combined to produce desired results. Many businesses have virtual partners in their supply chain because it is more flexible. An agile workplace moves ahead with the production of goods and services. It relies on feedback from relevant information and data. JIT (Just in Time) and TQM (Time Quality Management) are practices common in agile work environments. Others include information sharing and decision support systems and are normally related to a "lean" company (Soltan and Mostafa, 2015).

Agile organizations are required to react or respond to what is happening in the game. They are flexible enough to rewrite the long-term playbooks. They need to accept the premise of continual improvement. This implies that the business process has to be flexible enough to allow change and reaction to specific situations. This is supported by continuous improvement in business processes and the use of datamining technologies and AI (Brander et al, 2011).

Better education will help the adaption of AI but only under certain circumstances. Education itself will undergo a major change. Qualifications will be connected to the work and jobs. Roles like accountant will surely be done by intelligent software. As long as education teaches and promotes creativity and flexibility it will still be important. Expectations of employees will be greater but less rigid. Availability expectations will be much higher. Flexible hours and standby duties will be the rule, not the exception (Wisskirchen et al., 2017).

Cognitive and Task Agility

With AI and other intelligent technologies in the workplace, many jobs based on production or industrial processes will be eliminated. Big changes will need to be made. We need to move from the mindset of controlling a process to meeting a goal. The new concept is to support flexible design with the aim of delivering value. Agile started as a retaliation to inflexible and ineffective practices in the software industry. It has already gone far beyond those limitations. Changing corporate or organizational culture is hard. Making the change from a controlled process to a shared process involves including people in decisions. The shifts in workplace concepts will be anything but painless. Almost every job that requires an individual to process transaction data in front of a screen will be at risk. The critical criteria will be the level of routine. Machines will replace humans where the job process is repeated regularly and where the individual tasks can be made to be independent (Wisskirchen, et al., 2017).

Distributed cognition is a new way of looking at the workplace. It determines how work is performed. New work practices help us to look at distributed cognition. In the workplace cognitive agility means one person's connection to themselves and others. It includes the collective exchanges of groups of people. Both individual and collective cognition combine to create an expanded cognitive system. The individual's cognitive system is a single actor. It can include multiple other people and objects. Collectively distributed cognition involves multiple people's activities, objects and resources. Examples of this include either well-structured and functional or ill-structured and sloppy systems. Sloppy systems include processes, participants or objects that are either under- or over-specified. Both of these concepts come from classic cognitive science. This provides a framework to assess intelligence and problem solving.

Distributing work across groups requires breaking the work up into parts. This way people or agents can bring their expertise to subtasks within a larger business goal. The way information is represented in the workplace and then changed, combined and spread is, supposedly, in alignment with business goals. Problem solving can rely on one person or many people. Problems get solved with various degrees of reliability and efficiency. Intelligence then sits at the systems level in distributed cognition and can and does include AI. It also includes any other technologies that can support the idea of attaining business goals (Perry, 1999). Understanding this is key to the functioning of the workplace. This is true for both the individual and for the collective organization. Both knowledge and skills bring the organization together. This includes the individuals and subgroups that support the work environment.

Agile environments support continuous adaption of new tasks. This supports business processes and allows for flexible reactions in specific situations. In this way each case, each order, each customer has the ability to remain unique. KISS (Knowledge Intensive Service Support) is just one of many acronyms used for agile tasks. There will always be exceptions, unforeseen events, unpredictable situations, variations and complex tasks. "A task is a definition of a particular item of work. Tasks specify the requirements and the goal of that work"

(Brander, et al., 2011, p. 10). Different resources are used to accommodate different tasks. In an agile environment, the goal is to shorten the gap between the initial process design and the process execution. The most important principle of agile is to learn and adjust along the way (Mouser, 2015).

Many organizations will be faced with change or die scenarios and many workers will become unemployed. This will be exemplified where control and respective cognition and services have been the norm and where there is a resistance to adopting new ways of implementing business processes. Agile workplaces promise to be more people-focused, more flexible and more unique. This AI revolution is already here. The pace of adoptions is accelerating and the availability of opportunity to use and deploy technologies to support the workplace is speeding up. Agile paradigms have found their way into a multitude of workplaces alongside new supportive technologies changing roles and processes. From hospital emergency rooms to educational assessments, to budgeting and banking, sales calls and food processing, AI and new technologies are causing organizations to reinvent themselves. Big shifts have started to play out in industries as diverse as energy, healthcare, manufacturing and apparel, and more upheaval can be anticipated. Innovation and responsiveness will thrive while redundancy and predictive processes will be replaced, at least in part by new ways of working (Narayan, 2015).

Infrastructure and Obstacles

The pace of change is quickening. The speed of change is also accelerating. It is important companies have a plan for adopting and adapting to new technologies. This includes redefining business processes and employee roles. There are and will continue to be concerns in the new workplace with privacy and security. Because of the enormous amount of data collected and shared, privacy is a problem. The quality and safety risks are still largely undefined. The legal and regulatory issues could be substantial. Transformation to the agile workplace will not be easy. There will be tradeoffs. The cost and benefits of automating activities will fluctuate between augmenting and replacing different activities. The impact of intelligent machines will have an effect on the development of human skills and training. The pace of change requires organizations to accept these priorities. This will determine the competitive position of companies moving forward (Chui et al., 2015).

Changes that need to be considered involve inserted technology in a person's clothing. This is already happening in sports and wellness programs. AI is helping individuals keep track and benchmark their personal progress. This allows for comparison to others in their same age bracket or lifestyle. There is immense information available from health claims. Research may allow us to make suggestions for wellness, like in nutrition and medications. This data can also be used to relay real-time information to doctors or wellness experts. This may add to the future of a healthier workforce. We also see monitoring devices. Sometimes they use heartbeats or keystrokes and sometimes cameras. The devices used continue to be assessed on their own usefulness. AI will gather information and may even direct someone to a reliable and useful reference. A healthier workforce translates into a more productive and more cost-effective business.

These improvements in technology do not come without a price. Consider the privacy of the individual. Do they have the ability to "hold back" information (opt out)? Is it important to have that information provided to the business? Privacy legislation will be challenged across several fronts. First, to help business forge new territory. Second, the privacy rights of the employee or contingent worker to withhold information. It will not be a simple solution. Simply aggregating the information and eliminating the individual identifiers won't do it. AI will identify, assist and recommend actions at the micro-levels of the business. This will create improvements for the business because of the individual's information (Knight, 2018).

AI must be carefully programmed and monitored. It has the ability to increase inequalities in the workplace. And in the home, legal and judicial systems. Sexism, racism and other unrecognized biases can be built into machine-learning algorithms. The underlying intelligence will shape the way people are categorized and addressed. These risks perpetuate an already vicious cycle of bias. It could support, for example, systematic bias among poorer and nonwhite populations.

The truth is that most of the programming and data analytics are created globally by white males. Research by CMU shows that women are less likely than men to be shown ads on Google for executive jobs. Correlations to unrecognized biases can be supple and it can be dangerous. From pay scales to types of observation and surveillance, these algorithmic flaws are not easy to detect. Ingrained bias could easily be passed on to machine-learning systems and be built into the future. Intelligent machines could learn to think in ways that mirror a male dominated, narrow, privileged society which supports familiar prejudices and stereotypes (Crawford, 2016).

Far too often executives see only the short run. They don't deal with the magnitude of overall change. This is because the scale and scope are too much to handle. Change in small and large organizations can be overwhelming. Leading agile transformations in the workplace is challenging. Trying to compete in a new marketplace with technologies so advanced will be an even more enormous challenge. Leadership needs to take ownership. These technologies offer new challenges and opportunities. No one is going to get it all right all the time. Learning and adjusting as the organization moves through change and grows will be paramount.

Changes in the workplace will start at the enterprise level. This will happen with a commitment to continuous improvement in products and services. The first step is to organize and commit to clear business objectives. Next, to form a team that will lead the workplace with continuous improvement processes. Employees need to understand the importance of change. This is a new and agile work environment. They need to be engaged in all aspects of the process. They also need support with learning and development opportunities (Mouser, 2015).

The majority of CEOs, about 71%, are sure that the next few years will be more important than the last fifty (Wisskirchen, 2017, p. 21). Companies already use intelligent systems. This trend will continue to grow. Often there is difficulty in connecting new systems with established systems. A greater awareness of the employees' physical and cognitive activities can help when programming the systems. This is in the context of relevant tasks. Much work will need to be done to overcome the resistance to AI. Future workers will need the required AI skills. AI instills fear. This is usually of a plant or corporate closure. Employees will lose their jobs. In reality, it will be because of gross mismanagement. Workers fear massive job cuts and lack of retraining. Economics supports that labor is expensive and machines, once the original cost is overcome, are more competitive. Employees need to be involved in the development and process of change. They need to understand the implications of using new technologies and the future.

This will also cause upheaval in the education system. Future directions in education must support design thinking and encourage creativity. New curriculums will be designed to engage with the work. New degree programs will integrate with the creative work at the company. Adaptability is one of the major challenges humans will face. Those who can adapt to an agile environment will thrive. Those that cannot adapt will struggle. Employees must always be willing to learn new skills. The challenge for schools and colleges will be to teach students soft skills such as reliability, communication, social interactions, time management, accepting feedback and always, always continuing to learn (Wisskirchen, 2017).

Impact on Employee Perceptions

From the beginning, the concept and then the creation of AI has caused fear in the workplace. Stanley Kubrick's movie *2001*, with its evil computer Hal, exemplified the fears. AI could be a threat to human existence. AI is no longer on the horizon; in many areas it has arrived. In the short term, AI will not rival the Hal 9000 of Space Odyssey fame, but it could very easily and rapidly change the shape of the workplace. This has already begun. Clever Machines, robots, chatbots, smartbots and IOT have begun to infiltrate the work environment. By undertaking tasks done by humans they are capable of destroying millions of jobs almost overnight. Stephen Hawking believed that AI, much like the Internet, comes with challenges (Cellan-Jones, 2014). Elon Musk calls AI the most dangerous threat for humanity.

Bill Gates points out that AI could cause record unemployment very quickly. AI includes smart technology, artificial intelligence, robots, and algorithms (STARA). This could eliminate one-third of the jobs that exist today. Robots are improving a lot. This includes inexpensive self-governing units that can easily outperform humans. Examples include retail self-checkouts, smartphone applications, automated accounting, IOT, driverless cars and chatbots taking orders for fast food. The cost benefits to business are enormous. This makes it difficult to continue to consider humans in some roles moving forward.

Many of these jobs are high paying middle-class jobs and many of these jobs are in the service sector. Even those jobs that will not be eliminated will be disrupted by STARA. Many of these jobs will not be replaced. The highest incentive is to replace employees in the service sector. This is true because workers account for the largest overheads. This saves company money, lowers liability, and cuts costs. It's not just low paying jobs, but any job that can be routine enough to automate and simple enough to codify is susceptible to STARA (Brougham and Haar, 2017).

Changes in the Way We Work and Learn

This brings to light an entirely new perspective on how employers and educators must see jobs. And how learning and development needs to support employment. Careers need to be viewed as dynamic and borderless. We need to educate and train employees not for just one setting. Rather we need to train for dynamic, ever-changing and evolving work environments. These changes are wide and deep. They have huge implications for people at work. They have huge implications for how organizations will manage and compensate workers. Career satisfaction and turnover are just two of the many issues that will be affected by new technologies. This invasion of STARA will affect younger and older workers. The main impact of STARA will fall on those entering the workforce now and moving forward.

The implications for education are huge. Colleges, universities and training institutions need to understand the costs of education. Education needs to be about employment. As industries and economic sectors go into decline, educators need to focus on employment not on employability at a national and global level (Brougham and Haar, 2017). Employment is having the skills to get a job now. Employability is having the skills to maintain it and to gain upward mobility in your career.

Artificial Intelligence in Education (AIED) has changed and evolved. As STARA moves the workplace forward, these technologies need to be embedded in everyday lives. They need to support culture, practices, objectives and societies. Current classroom pedagogy needs to expand. It must include a wider partnership of learners with instructors. New technologies can support diversity and different content domains. The goal of education needs to move away from a definitive body of knowledge. It needs to move towards giving learners the tools to become adaptive experts and on the job learners. The curriculum must expand to include not just soft skills but knowledge application, teamwork and self-regulation.

Assessments too must change. They need to capture learning pathways and processes. Practices must include formative and summative assessments. They need to measure Just in Time support and authentic work elements. The movement will be toward supporting learning anytime and anyplace. It will not be restricted to a system or a structure. Teachers are no longer sages. They are guides to the integration of the technologies and applications. They lead the way for seeking, finding independent, collaborative thought. Learning will focus on authentic everyday tasks and challenges, context and actions. Embedding the learning in context will make it more relevant and real. Researchers must be bold and willing to take on new challenges. They need to take greater risks and tackle new contexts and domains. Interactive learning environments will be more than just domain knowledge. These environments will be built to support lifelong learning growth. They will support peer interactions, and act as intelligent tutors and perhaps mentors or life coaches (Wylie, 2016).

Lying in wait is the thought that learning is a skill to be taught. It is not just about learning a subject. Rather it is about analyzing the environment we live in and finding the problems that need solutions. This stretches learning to make us better problem solvers and innovators and not just experts in a discipline. With this comes a need to start training our newest generations in this lifelong learning experience. We must provide transition to the existing generations to "come up to speed." Learning is basically a closed loop process. It includes viewing, analyzing, changing, monitoring and looping back to viewing, continually. We must use technology like AI in our learning processes. This will assist in creating a closed loop system that is moving us and our businesses forward.

AI Enhanced Workplace Training

It is highly likely that people will need new environments for learning. New outcomes will not be geared to a degree or singular mastery of tasks. Rather they will reshape what we need to know and how/where to apply that knowledge. Current thinking puts soft skill learning into courses in preparation for the work environment. Businesses recognize that senior employees may not possess the leadership skills they need to move forward. Mentoring, team building, presenting and communicating are essential skills. Social skills and innovation are examples of what senior executives find lacking in the workforce.

Education will be enhanced when AI monitors processes and people. AI will be able to recommend changes to the environment to produce better outcomes. AI will collect information to help recognize the learning styles that produce the best results (Wang, 2018). And AI will find a home in the recruitment of staff based on assessments. It will use analysis to hire the most adaptable workers to fit the new workplace. AI has the ability to amass information for the purpose of recognizing patterns.

Recognizing potential success or harm provides companies with the ability to let training become self-directed. Companies will rely on AI to monitor the readiness of people, teams and the workforce for change.

AI can help to make the actions support success. It can temper conclusions by presenting additional information to support actions and decisions (Bennetts, 2018). Mobile apps combined with better voice recognition allow workers to access pertinent information. When and where they need "problem solving" they can find it on the "shop floor," in the field or even at home. With all the apps available, bringing teams together through mobile is easy. Introducing an AI team into the mix will result in faster problem resolutions. The future value of AI will be to propose new "problems" — things to think about — and measuring the outcomes. New scenarios will also be "crowd-sourced" to allow all areas of the business to contribute to a solution. AI combines solutions to problems to use as benchmarks for future problem solving.

What Our Future May Hold

AI will enhance the education process. It will be able to adapt, defuse knowledge faster and use visualization and more entertaining tools. Walmart is using VR (Virtual Reality) for training employees how to stock shelves and how to handle the Black Friday crowds (Thibodeau, 2018). Voice technology will be able to recognize different languages, dialects, and speech patterns. AI can access massive amounts of information to understand what is being asked. It can combine the information gathered from the device. As speech recognition improves, devices should provide privacy to an individual speaking to or hearing AI assisted learning. Unless this is mastered, we will only raise the "noise level" of our surroundings. This makes AI a less favorable method of communicating. The "hands-free" nature of speaking to our devices is very natural. It is a comforting way to introduce AI improvements to our lives. We already see the usefulness of such devices as Amazon Echo or Google Home. This, coupled with the IOT capabilities, allows us to talk to and gain insights from our devices. AI is sitting behind the scenes (Kanungo, 2018) (Sumser, 2018).

AI can benefit us immensely in areas of data integrity. Over the many years, we have progressively converted our information from one platform to newer platforms. This requires us to sometimes guess what the converted data really means. As a result, our business intelligence is tainted with erroneous or useless data. This is not because there is no need for that information. It is because the integrity of that data is highly suspect. AI can help reduce or even eliminate the problem. AI automation moves data input into the hands of those most directly involved with the transaction. It can ensure that the data is more reliable. It can compare the context where it is entered and make or suggest corrections. It can instantly create a better analysis of related data to make sure the data is highly accurate (Sutter, 2018).

AI will be at the center of global communities. It will generate ideas that are life altering. Using AI with crowd-sourcing information and aggregating it into thoughts and sharing it with the community can stimulate additional innovation. This puts us on a scale well outside of what we envision for just AI use in business. These communities will more than likely exhibit cross thinking. Global communities will share information and interact with AI on a scale that creates new thinking and ideas beyond what humankind has known. Newer thinking will be borne out of the AI process. Broader problem solving will become natural through cross-pollination. AI will be at the center of this, making us perhaps better humans. It may influence us to be more holistic. It may help us to solve global problems. AI may provide a stronger approach to the longevity of the entire human race.

The impact of AI in the workplace has enormous implications. AI is one of the most impactful technological advancements ever. It is far from being completely felt in our lives. If AI is not monitored and measured in terms of the costs to humans in the workforce, AI may well cause more chaos then advancement.

ASK THE HARD QUESTIONS

- What sectors of the economy are already being impacted by AI?
- How can businesses prepare to become agile?
- When will economic opportunity converge with technology in your industry?
- What prevents organizations from adapting easily to change?

Chapter 3

Disruption and Obsolescence

"Artificial intelligence will reach human levels by around 2029. Follow that out further to, say, 2045, we will have multiplied the intelligence, the human biological machine intelligence of our civilization a billion-fold."
—Ray Kurzweil

Change is what revolutions are all about. Change is the act or instance of making or becoming different. Revolutions are major, sudden and typically violent. They can change government, social structures or mean the complete 360 degree turnaround of a company. AI has the potential to have a revolutionary effect on the workplace. AI has the ability to have an impact on the world we live in that is greater than the industrial or digital revolution. Whether it's the influence on life span, automation, jobs being taken over by robots, the education system or the way we think, AI will be disruptive, and obsolescence is inevitable. The first signs of obsolescence can already be seen. The biggest devastation that AI will bring soon is job displacement. Millions of people will lose their jobs. Because of our lack of agility, awareness and planning, AI has the potential to harm a lot of people. It will disrupt the way we learn, the way we live and what has normally given a great deal of meaning and passion to our lives: our jobs (Brown, 2019).

The biggest and first influence of AI on our lives will be in the workplace. The impact will be more devastating and far-reaching than anything that came before it. This is because the effect will be spontaneous and because we live in an interconnected society. The digital revolution brought us big data. And the ability to buy goods and services from all over the globe. It brought us increased competition and new business models that changed entire industries. It also brought us increased wealth inequities and unemployment. Our challenge moving forward with AI is to use it to our advantage. This can happen by providing new products and services while increasing productivity. We need to create a plan for retraining, educating and creating new jobs and distributing wealth more equally.

Every innovative technology goes through the phase of discovery and then application. This is certainly true with AI. Research laboratories and universities are being replaced by entrepreneurs. New companies are putting the technology to practical use. AI is spreading all over the globe. AI has transitioned from the discovery phase to the deployment phase in the last 30 years. In the 1980s and 1990s we were still in the laboratories, discovering speech recognition and the Internet. The use of AI today is very different than the discovery of AI in laboratory settings. Changes will affect the infrastructure. The creation of new core technologies is mixed with operation details. AI is getting messy, sticky and more interesting every day. It's not just about the algorithms. It's about implementation. Implementation means BIG change. Changing infrastructure, creating new products and replacing old ways of doing things. Disruption and obsolescence are essentials for change (Makridakis, 2017).

AI Implementation and BIG Change

AI has moved quickly in the U.S. but even more quickly in China. The U.S. was heavily responsible for the research and innovation behind AI. China, because of its abundance of data and public infrastructure, is fertile ground for deployment of AI, especially in the workplace. AI plays right into the hyper-competitive atmosphere. China has also proven their ability to turn innovations into a wide range of practical and useful products that can go to market. The combination of innovation and practical implementation has, in a few short decades, taken AI from the laboratory into nearly every home. The Chinese have more than 1.1 billion smartphones, most of which have "Alexa." Apps like "We Chat" have fueled the data explosion. Chinese people use more apps than any other group of people on the planet.

Partly because they never adopted credit cards and partly because they didn't have the infrastructure that exists in Western countries. The medical systems, financial systems and shopping systems are ripe for jumping right into mobile phone apps. Using apps for everything provides more data. More data produces more insight for AI. AI companies can then tailor their products to the user (Lee, 2018).

There is a great deal of controversy over intellectual property theft between China and the U.S. But it's a little late for that. The horse has left the barn. Commercial adoption of AI is here. China has proven that mobile apps can replace a great deal of the infrastructure we currently have in place. China has been very good at exploring and exploiting the possibilities of AI. The cultural attitude of "if it works copy it" has created a fiercely competitive environment. China excels at taking what works and quickly adapting it to new markets or tweaking it to make it better. If a Chinese company moves quickly it survives and grows, if it is slow to adapt it dies. Agility is the key to surviving.

The deployment of AI comes with considerable risk. China also has a strong government investment in AI. They have a very different attitude toward change in infrastructure and privacy issues. This risk is felt in many areas and one of the most significant is personal privacy. AI researchers can't do research on cancer without available patient records, and autonomous vehicles can't function without road sensors. The Chinese government has sent the signal to local governments to make the changes necessary to adopt AI. China has made AI a top priority.

How this will all play out remains to be seen. Both America and China can and should look toward the workforce. It's time to get out of the clouds and realize it is not just about hands-off innovation. It's not just about taking a proven idea and tweaking and commercializing it. Both countries are creating and breaking new ground. They are also developing a variety of combinations for deploying many different forms of AI. It's time to get going and understand the implications on humans and how they work (Lee, 2018).

Now is the time to wake up! We need to get smarter about what's happening with AI. AI now comes to us in the form of chips embedded in IOT using mostly speech recognition and natural language processing. It is in your car, refrigerator and light fixtures. It is part of your surveillance cameras and part of your email inbox. AI has a positive and negative side. The positive side will help us live smarter, work smarter and create healthier and safer work environments. But the potential for hacks, malicious use and abuse are real. AI has and will continue to disrupt all industries. It will affect the workplace locally and globally. There is no doubt unemployment will increase and no doubt that AI will make our lives easier.

Automated application development has gone mainstream. AI meets DevOps (Development and Operations). Data is created by using AI technologies. Quality is taking the place of sheer quantity with the data provided for AI. Companies are springing up with the sole purpose of cleaning up unstructured "Big Data" and making it into more usable "Little Data." Natural language processing has made it easier for machines to talk to humans and humans to talk to machines. Building on these capabilities, computers can discern understanding, and capture sentiment, meaning and intent. By combining what computers do best (machine learning, deep learning, language processing, understanding, forecasting and optimization), the reach of AI continues to grow. AI can chart changes in account spending or forecast energy consumption or weather patterns. AI is getting better and better. We use it to classify, group and arrange data about everything. AI helps us understand X-rays and can determine if the nodes on a scan are benign or malignant. AI can transcribe speech to text. AI offers us shopping suggestions, generates reports and summarizes results. All AI requires data. AI is only as good and dependable as the programming that went into it and the data that supports it.

AI is Replacing Boundaries

AI has already impacted the workplace positively. AI technologies will play an even larger role moving forward. There will be more change and disruption in the next five years than there has been in the last twenty. This is because the population entering the workforce is demanding it. Training and career development are increasingly important. Employees expect new learning opportunities to go along with salary and benefits. Flexibility, both in location and changing job roles, goes hand in hand with the agile workplace. Geographical boundaries replaced by technologies allow for collaboration and productivity from anywhere. This saves the company money. It improves the lifestyle of the employee. It also changes the way we onboard and support our workforce. This is where AI comes in to play.

An estimated 37 billion dollars is waisted annually because new employees don't understand their jobs. The four "Cs" of onboarding – compliance, clarification, culture and connection – are what help new employees to be productive and engaged. Having a personal assistant help you through this process is invaluable. AI assistants are enabling new hires and employees that change jobs or transfer locations to understand their roles quicker and better. AI can build confidence by helping ease the disruption innate in new environments, new people and new roles. Flying people around the globe for training and onboarding has become obsolete. By 2025 young people will make up 75% of our workforce. Technology has always been a part of most millennials' lives. Technology is going to play a larger role in attracting and retaining this talent. AI is helping us connect and train workers (Cornerstone, 2018).

Changes to the Way We Learn

A college degree is not what it used to be in the workplace. The agile workplace requires training and retraining, learning and relearning, new skills, new knowledge and new attitudes. The job roles and skills needed are rapidly changing just like the technologies that support them. The faster technologies move, the greater the skills gap and the more important constantly having new opportunities to learn becomes. When asked, Henry Ford said, "If I had asked people what they wanted, they would have said faster horses." Our adaption of technologies into the world of education so far has been exactly that, faster horses. Disruption is not about faster horses. Real revolution is coming and the way we teach and learn will dramatically change (Househ, 2018).

We cannot compete with machines, but we shouldn't have to. So far little disruption has occurred in education. We have created online course rooms, eLearning classes and virtual worlds with online campuses. Second Life is a perfect example of schools spending millions of dollars to recreate their face-to-face buildings in a virtual environment. Human tutoring so far has been the gold standard in education. All this is about to change and change rapidly. The disruption will come in both the learning and development space and traditional education. All learning will change when we break through barriers and build interactive learning environments (ILEs). ILEs will let us individualize the learning and put it where we need it.

We have begun to see this in Virtual Reality (VR) and with Virtual Assistants (VA) on the job. Thanks to the volumes of data both active and ambient learning has become a science. ILEs are engineered to support the learner but also to collect and analyze data so that AI can help us learn how we learn. Whether it is a computer, handheld device, robot or wearable, AI is helping us analyze how and what people learn and why. Experimentation in various content domains, various education processes, self-regulation, resilience and grit, collaboration and motivation are just a few of the insights AI is starting to provide. Will traditional classroom environments become obsolete? Probably. Certainly, education is one field that will experience widespread disruption. The more we learn about learning science using AI, the more we will be able to construct ILEs that support those principles.

Transform Not Disappear

Obsolescence and disruption come to us with great promise, vast improvements in productivity, freedom from heavy and boring work and an improved quality of life. To state that all jobs, organizations and educational institutions are becoming obsolete is misleading. But it is not an understatement to say the future of work is change. At least this is true for most occupations. What will change and how soon are work processes. Certain activities will be automated, and this will require entirely new business processes. Jobs will transform rather than disappear. AI automation means a loss of approximately 2 trillion dollars in wages annually. This will affect all levels of wage earners. The benefits of AI so greatly outweigh the costs that organizations will have to adapt (Chui et al., 2015).

Lawyers, real estate agents, doctors, salespeople and every other occupation you can think of will be changed by AI. Some lower wage occupations are less vulnerable including home health care aides, plumbers, landscapers, maintenance crews and groundskeepers. How dramatic will this impact be? That depends on who you talk to! Some reports indicate that about 60% of current jobs could have at least 30% or more of their role automated. Most occupations will be affected significantly. The emphasis will shift from longer hours worked to work of higher value. Sadly, so little of what happens in the workplace requires true creativity or human emotional connection. This is about to change. The pace of transformation is picking up as more AI finds its way into our daily lives. Obsolescence and disruption are fueled by the speed that these technologies are being adapted. It is in directly related to the agility of the organization. Agile organizations can and will redefine roles, adapt new processes and change culture and mindset.

Humans become even more important in a world upended by technology. Maximizing productivity requires more than just hiring warm bodies. Attrition and turnover, issues that have plagued companies for years, are front and center. Organizations will need to change their mindset. They will need to not only hire the best people for the job, but also train and retrain them to keep them as engaged and as productive as possible. AI use for recruiting, engagement and retention is an area where technology has the ability to bring humanity back into the workplace. The days of Human Resources just hiring, doing annual reviews and going through the motions is outdated. Productivity is a marriage between technologies and human talent able to determine when to intervene (Farrow, 2018).

Economics and Disruption

Obsolescence and disruption effect economics. Most organizations will face significant change in the next decade. The economics of automation and AI includes exploring the tradeoffs. This includes replacing vs. expanding various roles. It also includes implications for human talent in the organization (Chui, et al., 2015). Another influence on the workforce is age. There is no reason why a workplace with workers in their 50s and 60s can't be as innovative. But age seems to slow down the adoption of new technologies and change. The median age of a worker is now 42 years old. Twenty years ago, the median age was 38. In the last several decades we have reshaped life expectancy, and this has implications for work. The aging of the population is challenging economic structures from Social Security to Medicare. America is getting old. Our labor supply is shrinking. Baby boomers are retiring, and a great deal of knowledge is going with them. This challenges the redefinition of roles and processes.

By 2030 only 59% of adults over 16 will be in the workforce. This influences economic wellness for each and every person. Older workers may be less likely to adapt to change. They may not be used to learning new skills, so businesses with older workers may be less agile, less likely to deploy emerging technologies. About half of American companies are 11 years old or older. Robots and AI could help companies address some of this disparity. It might seem counterintuitive but by replacing retiring workers, AI might help fill a worker shortage and raise productivity and incomes. The aging workforce becoming obsolete isn't often examined. Replacement by technologies may be something that allows us to age out of the workplace gracefully. For all the fear and misgivings about AI and robots, technologies might have a very positive effect on a workforce that is quickly aging out (Porter, 2019).

New Technologies Are Arriving Daily

Innovative technologies are coming to the workplace at increasing rates. Every day new technologies are being tweaked into some new application. Applications that teach interviewing, collaboration, conversation and coaching skills are delivered as games, eLearning and videos. Successful organizations are trying to sort through this explosion of apps. They want products that will support organizational performance. Successful organizations learn to focus on solutions not on technologies. The business environment is increasingly complex.

It's not a question of if AI will make it into our workplace but how. There is a lot of hype and fear generated around AI. AI will offer us practical solutions to many issues. Leadership will make all the difference in how AI affects a particular industry, segment or workplace. Changing business processes requires bold vision and transparency that all stakeholders can grasp. It will be a balancing act between business objectives, economic reality and the ethical implications of the impact on people. People are and always will be the most valuable resource of any organization. By improving what people are good at and minimizing their shortcomings, leadership will find a way to integrate AI into the business equation. AI can be used to strengthen our workplaces. AI can make them safer, more reliable and more productive, and improve the way we live and work (SAS, 2018).

AI will continue to learn, and machine learning will continue to automate complex tasks and interact with us in ways that can be termed intelligent. AI will continue to take in and analyze information, make assessments and evolve. Deep learning will continue to learn from data, using patterns and algorithms. The implications of analyzing and making inferences from extremely large amounts of data without getting tired is what computers do best. What humans do best is strategy.

Computers don't understand strategy. The analysis performed by computers is limited to tasks, performed very quickly and extremely accurately. Computers are also limited in scope and therefore can only provide limited insight. They are excellent at performing redundant and repetitive tasks but not so great at taking the results and determining what role those results will play as part of a larger strategy. AI has both strengths and weaknesses. It is our job as humans to understand both sides of the equation. This way humanity can benefit from and not be blindsided by the economic disruption. Leadership can help us harness the benefits if we can learn lessons from the past. Hard lessons. Lessons on how obsolescence and disruption have caught us off guard and how we can be aware and awake now.

This is not the first time humanity has experienced dynamic change caused by new technology.

We are currently using AI in the banking industry to identify fraud, credit risk and make market suggestions. We are using it in law enforcement to catch criminals, and in government to create smart cities. In health care and medicine, we are using it for diagnostics, monitoring and imaging. In energy and manufacturing we are using it to optimize the supply chain and for forecasting. In retail and communications, we are using AI to personalize shopping and replace redundant tasks. In all these sectors obsolescence and disruption are all too real.

No one knows exactly how AI will affect our society. It is nearly impossible to foresee the future. But what we can do is learn from the past. In this case we only need to look at the recent past to see that successful companies can disappear overnight. Entire sectors can morph and vanish. Products that were successful, and we relied upon, no longer exist. What is unique about this point in history is speed. Time to adoption, speed of obsolescence and scope of disruption have the potential to impact us beyond anything humanity has previously experienced. In Sapiens: A Brief History of Humankind, Yuval Noah Harari explores the agricultural, industrial and scientific revolutions. One can't help but see the increasing speed of change. How AI will affect industries, organizations, products and positions will depend on what humans have learned from the past and how we prepare for the future.

ASK THE HARD QUESTIONS

- What can leadership do now to identify the impact of AI?
- How has AI impacted the workplace in a positive way?
- What occupations are at high risk for obsolescence and disruption?
- What differences exist between younger and older workers that will be impacted by AI?
- Can AI help companies with knowledge transfer? How?

Google, the biggest of "Big Data," didn't really have AI until 2012. It was built into Google's search engine since the beginning. But it wasn't until a team from Google engineered 16,000 processors in 1,000 computers, making 1 billion connections, that AI at Google started to imitate the human brain. The human brain is capable of more than a trillion connections. The rest is history. Google had a neural network and humanity had a search engine that was teaching itself to think. If you live anywhere on the planet except China, Google is probably your search engine. Google was on the same journey we are all on, one that we don't really understand. We do know, however, it is extremely important. AI launched a new dimension in technologies. One that means anything we get right or wrong will have enormous impact on humanity (Brooker, 2019).

Smart chatbots and vocally activated technologies are everywhere. Some are good, some are not so good. They are easy to make and getting better. These devices help us hire babysitters and function as lawyers. They are taking jobs and will have a massive impact on the workplace and employment. Although they offer the potential for opening new positions and roles, what and how this will all play out has yet to be determined. Undoubtably, there will be upheaval and redefinition of workplace performance (Hirsch, 2017).

The IBM 360/75 was the mainframe computer of its day. In 1969 it helped to land our first astronauts on the moon. It had 6 megabytes of computing power. Today that equates to 10% of the computing power needed for the game Candy Crush. In 2001

Chapter 4

From Great to Gone

**"Every major industry was once a growth industry.... In every case, the reason growth is threatened, slowed, or stopped is not because the market is saturated. It is because there has been a failure of management."
—Theodore Levitt**

So Much Computing Power

IBM's Watson played Jeopardy against humans and Watson won.

This fast growth in computing power has led to factory floors populated by robots and not just at Tesla. In 2017, Apple's supplier Foxconn replaced 60,000 workers with robots in a factory in China. Amazon continues to roll out robot-staffed warehouses and distribution centers. Most of the activity at shipping ports, from Los Angeles to Baltimore, is now done by robots. Even law enforcement has gone robotic. Security robots patrol the parking lot, while high speed bots chase down criminals. Robots are building houses, aiding the military, delivering pizza and making meals at McDonald's. They are helping to drive cars and soon trucks, play music and turn lights off and on.

There are lessons to learn from the past if we are willing to look. Lessons where entire sectors of the economy disappeared. These organizations are on top of their game one day and gone the next. Products that dominated the marketplace vanished. Technology, music, retail, steel, communications, transportation, photography, energy and appliances; all have something to share. What's different about obsolescence with the arrival of AI is the speed. Entire sectors will feel the impact quickly, and entire segments of the labor force will become unemployed. Once the effect is felt, it is already late in the game. Change needs to come early, before the disruption, with education, training, foresight and planning. Transitioning to the agile workplace is possible with preparation. The foresight falls on leaders; the implementation is up to individuals.

What causes things to become obsolete? In the transportation industry, cars replaced horses and planes replaced trains. Technical innovation, change of location, finance or the next big thing can be the instigator. Whatever triggers disruption, what is important is the ability to react quickly. AI is already affecting multiple segments in the global economy. Accounting, transportation, healthcare, banking, insurance, coding, government, manufacturing, legal, mining, defense and retail are only a few of the segments in danger. Education, communication, media, hospitality, entertainment, sports, agriculture, and real estate are a few more. AI is creating music, analyzing performance and targeting advertising. The longer AI is here, the more the influence of AI will be realized, and the impact is deep.

Big Computer Companies... Vanished!

Technical innovation is usually what is blamed for obsolescence. The culprit is really the failure of sectors, organizations and people to react to it in a timely manner. The computer industry in the 1980s and 1990s is a perfect example of sector obsolescence. The minicomputer started a revolution in technology. It gave us smaller, faster and more individualized processors. It dominated the industry for about twenty years. Then it was replaced by servers and the personal computer. Digital Equipment Corporation (DEC), Data General (DG) and Wang Laboratories are examples of an economic sector that vanished. Two of today's big players in AI, IBM and Apple, almost went with them. What happened and what can we learn?

DEC began in 1957 and focused on the small end of the market with very little competition. The PDP series in the 1960s and 1970s cemented their place in the sector. They remained the second largest employer in Massachusetts next to the state government. The VAX 11 series put them into competition with the IBM 370s and was the first 32-bit machine. More powerful 32-bit computers came along. By the early 1990s DEC was in big trouble. They tried a 64-bit computer, but the evolution in chip production by Intel and others quickly surpassed any of the efforts by DEC. DEC was acquired in 1998 by Compaq. Compaq was a personal computer manufacturer who had no idea what to do with DEC. They also got into financial trouble. Compaq was eventually acquired by Hewlett-Packard (HP) in May 2002.

There are many explanations for the fall of the tech giant, DEC. DEC was clearly focused on competing with IBM on the high end of the market. The market sector had shifted to low end personal computers. How did they not see this? IBM almost missed it too. There was clear frustration with the leadership for failure to give clear vision and guidance on how to move forward. Most of these organizations were vertical. The movement was toward a more horizontally organized company. The BUNCH – Burroughs, Univac, NCR, CDC and Honeywell – were all vertically orientated. Vertical structure can be anything but agile. Customers began to lose faith and leadership changes – like Ken Olsen being dropped in 1992 and Bob Palmer being instated – didn't help. Olsen thought his product was so good, DEC did not need to pay sales commissions. The product would sell itself. The competition, IBM, paid very healthy commissions. Gordon Bell, DEC's technical guru, left because he was unable to pursue a personal computer and X-Windows strategy. Some would argue it was when Bell left that DEC, which was an engineering company, lost its hero. Still others report a serious lack of strategy as the problem.

DEC went from industry giant to gone. The myth that better technology is always the way to win in the market space was debunked. At one time DEC had the best processor, the best search engine and the best computers. Engineering was on their side, but timing was not. By the time DEC had the EXP chip, Intel had the chip market. DEC created the VAX but held on to the VAX too long. DEC looked at the Apple II but missed the opportunity to innovate. When it finally came to market with a PC it was years late and overpriced. Years later, DEC cut a deal with Apple to put the Apple OS on all DEC computers, but it never happened. The war between Silicon Valley and Boston's Rte. 128 with DEC, DG and Wang had yet to play out. Culture wins out in the end, again. Who was more agile? Silicon Valley had thousands of little startups and Boston had a few big self-contained firms (Peiffer, 2011; Goodwin, 2016; Malone, 2000). Then of course there was the attitude "We're too big to fail."

Too Big to Fail

DEC was not the only large computer company to fail. Neighbors on Boston's high-tech highway, Wang Laboratories succumbed to the rapid changes in high tech. Thirty-six-year-old CEO Fred Wang famously said billion-dollar companies don't disappear overnight. Then that's exactly what Wang did (Malone, 2000). Wang was a family company. It went public but kept the leadership in the family.

During the 1970s Wang led innovation in the computer industry and was primarily responsible for putting computers into offices. A computer in the office in the early 1970s was rare. The Wang 2200 was widely used in laboratories and healthcare. It was aggressively marketed and hardwired. Wang made two decisions that made it less agile: Wang decided to concentrate on hardware, not software, and to focus on word processors and minicomputers, not PCs (Goldstein, 2017).

Wang did shift product lines from calculators to word processors to computers, and in the end, went after IBM and the high end of the market. However, although leadership chased IBM, lack of sales and customer training limited Wang's reach. When Microsoft and the PC came out, no one needed a minicomputer to do word processing and the market collapsed. Egos got in the way of leadership. An Wang, the company's founder, refused to develop an IBM-compatible PC because he didn't like IBM. Wang wasn't listening to the market and wasn't able to adjust. Although death took a while, Wang filed for bankruptcy in 1992. Wang stock traded for $42 and dropped to $.50. Wang failed to listen to customers. Wang was a closed organization that had isolated leadership. They were unable to respond to market changes with a new direction for the company. Wang hung on to a culture of proprietary technology when the world was embracing open systems. Other companies, a bit more agile, like HP, IBM and Apple were able to survive but not without struggle and reorganization (Silverthorne, 1992).

Wang is a notable example of obsolescence and disruption. Unable to move past leadership troubles, slow declines turned into fast declines and, poof, they were gone. Certainly, there are questions of nepotism and whether Wang should have remained basically a family business. An Wang's ego played a big part in the inability to be agile and move in a new direction. When he insisted his son, Fred, take over as leader, shares that topped the $800 mark lost $424 million. That is a near 50% loss in a single fiscal year. When

Wang filed for bankruptcy in 1992, the company was over $500 million in debt. (Smith, E. 2017; L.A. Times, August 19, 1992).

Data General (DG) survived a little longer but not much. Data General also disappeared. EMC, a very large storage company, bought DG. Edson deCastro, one of four founders, had left DEC to establish Data General in 1968 (Computer History Museum, 2019). In 1969 DG released the Nova minicomputer. It quickly became a popular machine with science and education markets. They were the punk rockers of the minicomputer era, known for competitive management style and menacing technical vision. After a long struggle in one hardware market or another, they too were unable to be agile enough to transition to the PC era.

Famous for their engineering, the crew that made DG a company of innovation jumped ship in the early 1980s. They saw the handwriting on the wall. Minicomputers were out and the PC was in. Twenty years ago, The Soul of a New Machine by Tom West talked about the inner workings of high-tech leadership. Tom was a top engineer at DG, and a project leader. The book discusses territorialism, leadership motivations, revelations and devotion. It talks about protecting resources, political wars and burnout. It tells the story of building the Eagle MV/8000 mini-supercomputer, and why DG was split up between Massachusetts, the original home, and Research Triangle in North Carolina. (There were tax issues with the governor.) It talks about bitter internal competition and authoritarian leadership styles. The Eagle was supposed to save DG, but it didn't. DG lost market share to DEC and the rest is history (Ratliff, 2000).

Markets Change

Hardware vendors tried to lock the customer in or make it expensive and hard to switch vendors. Then the market changed. No one really cared about the hardware anymore. The new draw was the ability to run third party software. Changes in MySQL and software development caused changes in the hardware markets. Vendors fixed on service contracts and hardware upgrades began to vanish. High speed storage was not part of the minicomputer world. When Apple and IBM jumped into PC power architecture and Motorola picked up the manufacturing contract, these moves stuck a dagger in DG, too.

Proprietary hardware was becoming obsolete and so was DG. In 1988, DG leadership, led by Tom West, put together a report indicating they needed a heavy investment in software, or they could not compete with IBM and DEC. DG needed to get out of the proprietary hardware business. Instead of trying to compete with these two larger companies, DG would try to make commodity machines and run UNIX software. That worked for a while. Vendor lock in the computer market was over and the customer had won. DG didn't vanish into bankruptcy but was gobbled up in a takeover by EMC in 1999. EMC stopped all production of hardware and was sold to Dollar General in 2009. The last member of the Massachusetts Miracle (DEC, Wang and DG) met its demise in 1999.

What happened to these giants of technology? DEC failed to anticipate the PC and was bought by Compaq, which was bought by HP. Wang made minicomputers, trying to compete with IBM on the high end, but the word processor division was the money maker. DG bet the ranch on proprietary hardware and lost. EMC, a storage company, acquired

DG, merged with Dell (a story in itself) and EMC was eventually sold to Dollar General. All three companies had serious leadership issues. All three were anything but agile. All three had chances to survive but made serious strategic mistakes (Ross, 2018).

Both IBM and Apple struggled in the 1990s but were able to survive and even thrive. Although they were technology leaders that fell from glory, both were able to reinvent themselves. iPods, smartphones and mobile saved Apple. The Cloud saved IBM. It is worth studying their business decisions, their ability to react to technical changes, customer reactions, company size, culture and agility. Apple, the darling of big technology companies, took the world by storm in 1977 with the Apple II. It was the first successful personal computer. The Mac was the next big technological advance. It defined a GUI (Graphical User Interface) and all personal computers since the Macs have used it. The Apple MAC redefined how personal computers work. But by the mid 1990s the culture at Apple had changed. Deadlines, new release dates and deliverables had morphed into a research mentality, and they were not motivated by profits. Apple was falling on hard times. Apple came to market with a few products that didn't make it, the Apple III, Lisa, Mac 128k, the Mac OS and AOCE. They were up against Windows. Microsoft dominated the business PC market.

One of the most familiar and famous failures at Apple was the Apple Open Collaborative Environment (AOCE). It was a project that went out of control. The software application was a memory monster and a diskspace and bandwidth hog. Apple failed to execute on upgrading the processing quality of its Operating System and then Windows arrived. Apple management did a lot of stupid things, including charging more for products that seemed to provide less than the competition. Apple pulled out of this near demise with the iPod, a move away from the PC market. Microsoft had 90% of the PC market. The rest is history.

IBM had its share of trouble before its rebirth in 1993. Louis Gerstner took over top management from John Akers and then engineered a turnaround still respected today. IBM led the computer industry for decades but suffered financial losses from their peak $68.9 billion in 1990 to $5.9 billion in 1993. It was like the fall of the Roman Empire. Incompetent leaders, massive amounts of wasted resources, and rivals springing up all around them. IBM had stayed focused on mainframes and divided up into "Baby Blues." The mainframe market was shrinking and drying up quickly. Instead of focusing on innovation, IBM focused on more production. The market was changing from higher priced low-volume computers to lower priced high-volume offerings. IBM bet the ranch on mainframes and mainframes were being replaced. IBM management kept trying to do the same old thing, dominate and control. When IBM finally came to market with a PC, it signed very controversial contracts with both Microsoft and Intel. These contracts did not prohibit either of these companies from selling to IBM competitors. IBM had become a mismanaged bureaucracy. It took Louis Gerstner to return to the founder's mentality of Watson, Sr., which was "IBM is in one business of meeting customer need for information processing" (Singh, 2006).

Changing the Status Quo

Clayton Christensen classifies technologies as sustaining or disruptive. Existing companies, it seems, have difficulty dealing with disruptive technologies. A great deal of this is based on company culture and management. Disruptive technologies do exactly that, they disturb, unsettle, upset the status quo. AI is a disruptive technology. Blaming only top management for failures is too simple. Loss of key personnel can also contribute. Often it is a combination of changes. New technologies and internal stagnation cause confusion. In other words, even if the company knows it needs to make changes, changes are impossible to implement. The organization's culture, rigid structure and lack of agility don't change overnight (Vasil, 2006).

Retail has been feeling the effects of disruptive innovation for years. Innovation and market changes present challenges to department stores and "Big Box" retailers. Department stores that were part of our history and childhood, for anyone over 30, have disappeared. Very few department stores will survive. Kaufmann's, which was founded in Pittsburgh in 1871, closed its doors in 2006. Gimbles, another predominant department store in Pittsburgh, PA... gone. In 1974 Hess's, a regional store in the Northeast, had a similar fate. Hechinger is another fatality. Filene's Department Stores, a Boston based chain acquired by Macy's... also gone. Hess's, Hecht's, Hills, Abraham & Straus, Bonwit Teller, Bon-Ton, Ames, Mervyn's, Caldor, Rich's, Wanamaker's, Foley's and E. J. Korvette are all gone, and this is not an inclusive list. Even Macy's is in dire straits and on the way out. How did this happen to an entire industry sector? What changed? Some experts blame it on geographics and the move to the suburbs; others would go straight to Amazon.

Big box retailers and retail chains have also been severely impacted. Blame it on convenience of shopping in your pajamas. Some tried to adapt to e-commerce and new technologies and didn't make it. Kmart, JCPenny, Sears, and Toys "R" Us disappeared or are disappearing right before our eyes. Electronic retailers like Circuit City, Radio Shack and CompUSA vanished. Beloved bookstores including Borders Books, B. Dalton, and Walden... are all gone. And many, many more: Linens 'n Things, H. H. Gregg, Gadzooks, the Discovery Channel Store, Sharper Image, Sports Authority, The Limited, Kids "R" Us... Gone. And the list goes on. The purpose of this reflection is not a walk down memory lane, but rather to emphasize how entire sectors like retail can be impacted by change. Many businesses also fall into this category. How can great industries leaders like Bethlehem Steel Corporation, Gulf Oil, Newsweek, MCI, Pan American Airlines, Continental Airlines and Kodak just disappear? The answer is complicated.

Yet, other companies are changing retail because they have chosen to innovate. Chains like Ultra Beauty changed the model by putting beauty services in the store. Adidas began 3D printing for sneakers and Blue Apron is bringing restaurant meals to the kitchen. Even Walmart showed its agility by making huge investments in e-commerce and online retail. One of the most iconic of the new breed in retail is Warby Parker, which changed the way we buy eyewear. There are many other examples of organizations that managed to see things differently and innovate. Of course, no one innovates like Amazon. They have a hand in everything.

In 2012 Amazon bought a robotics company, Kiva Systems. It introduced stores with no cashiers.

Amazon Go replaced many human jobs with thousands of robots in the distribution and fulfillment sector. Delivery with drones is on the horizon. Retail stores with no cashiers are approaching quickly. Walmart, another giant in retail, is using robots to stock shelves and scrub floors. Even Kroger has automated warehouse facilities with robotic capabilities. AI, robots and automation are at the point that they can deliver both technically and economically. The impact on the workplace is inevitable. Good jobs will be replaced by the automation and the initiative will be driven by the profit motive. It's all about economics.

Productivity has always been directly linked to employment. This is changing and changing dramatically. In some cases, automation is replacing unpleasant and difficult tasks. It is assisting workers so that they can better serve customers. The statistics are not on the side of the worker. In 2017, Reuters found that stores currently employed fewer people than they did ten years before. In the next twenty years the retail landscape will look very different than it ever has in the past. Even if robotics and AI create new jobs, it will take additional training in the workplace to ensure people have the skills to move quickly into new roles and occupations. About 3.4 million people were employed as retail cashiers as of 2018. It is unclear what these people will do. Will they be retrained when robots take over retail? (Melendez, 2018).

Most people think of robots in the warehouse but that's not all robots and AI can do! There are applications in retail far beyond just stocking shelves and filling orders. Robots can sell things, spot mistakes in pricing or stocking, monitor inventory levels, and help shoppers find things. Robots can minimize theft and they can be available 24/7 with built in security (Matthews, 2018). Robots and AI offer a wealth of opportunities to the retail sector, including cutting costs and increasing quality of service.

Traditionally retail meant a physical store. Today retail has multiple touchpoints. It has seamless service with products delivered right to your door. Augmented and virtual reality technologies are playing an increasing role in retail. Smart mirrors, in stores or at home, keep the customer from having to try on clothing, giving comparative feedback for fit and 360 degree views. The more digital we become, the fewer physical stores matter. Online technologies, mobile and other consumer interfaces keep evolving. Physical showrooms that lead to online purchasing is one example of how retail is evolving. Warby Parker and Bonobos are just two examples. Customers can come in and try on products, find the perfect fit, and then have it shipped to their doorstep.

A McKinsey report indicates that 800 million people will lose their jobs to robots by 2030. Collecting and processing data can be done better, faster and cheaper by machines (Holley, 2019). If we look at the past, we can see the extent of digital disruption. Tower Records serves as a perfect example of unexpected and unprepared obsolescence. Organizational obsolescence includes media giants like Newsweek, industrial magnets like Bethlehem Steel, communication giants like MCI and technology powerhouses, Blackberry, VisiCalc, Sunbeam, Blockbuster, WordPerfect, Palm, Altair, Commodore, Atari.

Of course, this discussion of "From Great to Gone" would not be complete without mentioning Kodak, the company that dominated the photography business for over 100 years. Founded by Eastman in 1888 until its bankruptcy filing in 2012, Kodak was an industry giant. Much like the other companies mentioned, it now exists like a ghost of its former self. Many companies are gone. Some still exist as shadows. In all cases, lack of agility, management mistakes and technology innovations played a big role. Management needs to act now to save or re-create the jobs of tomorrow. In every case when an industry is threatened, slowed or stopped, it is because management failed (Levitt, 2004).

ASK THE HARD QUESTIONS

- What industries does AI threaten now? Ten years from now?
- How will finance affect AI innovation?
- How will AI affect the customers?
- How do we act quickly enough to benefit from AI?
- How do we avoid or adapt to massive unemployment?

AI is making recommendations, suggesting alternatives and translating languages. The news we receive daily is produced and presented by some form of bot, not a human being. It is taking over the role of human advisor. Any field based on historical research, known strategies, models and basic review and analysis is vulnerable. What are the keys? Standard and recurring questions and significant data for AI to work with. Any field that relies on data for superior strategies and insight will have AI as part of the workplace.

No one starts out to replace people with AI. Technologies are used to solve human problems and enhance business processes. In the past the only way we had to deliver expertise was people. In the future data will tell us. That's what makes clean data so very important. Data is what drives AI. AI covers a very wide range of applications. Part of the challenge is the definition we've placed on AI. AI has taken on the scope of replacing human thought. Once we understand AI, it is just another software application. Another tool in the technology arsenal to solve another business problem. It's important that humans have a clear understanding of how AI works.

Confidence in AI relies on confidence in the data. Often AI makes decisions and predictions based on varying degrees of certainty. AI helps business in anything involving numbers and data like billing, pricing and marketing. The more predictable the task, the less inherent uncertainty involved, the quicker AI can generate accurate responses as long as the data cooperates. Often AI is seen as a black box. But it's not a question of whether AI is more accurate than

Chapter 5

Disappearing Jobs and the Future

"Whatever affects one directly, affects all indirectly."
—Martin Luther King Jr.

humans, it is a question of whether AI is as accurate as humans.

AI will impact most industries. Most AI applications for the workforce currently are concerned with process, procedure, workflow improvement or replacement. AI also requires new kinds of talent. Engineers, programmers, analysts and other AI related professionals are part of the package whether they are in-house or contract. Oftentimes in order to address human needs, AI can't just be dropped into place. It has to be installed. AI needs to adapt and then adjustments made. Employing AI is often a disturbing and resisted process (Thomsen Reuters, 2020).

What does all this mean for humans that work for a living? It means we have to get smart. The disruption is already here. The impact on jobs is already enormous. Brick and mortar stores are disappearing, and retail jobs are becoming a thing of the past. Online retailers use AI to not only provide potential customers with data driven suggestions but also to deliver purchases to their doorstep. The supply chain is optimized online. Browsing history and purchasing recommendations have been able to optimize supply and demand in a way face to face retailing never achieved.

As old jobs vanish, new ones are created. Retail service jobs are down, and light trucking and delivery services are up. It turns out we haven't stopped shopping; we still want consumer goods. New jobs are springing up to support new business models. When autonomous cars and trucks hit the market, delivery jobs and trucking jobs will change. Job creation and job destruction are both on the horizon for most if not all industries. The real question is what kinds of jobs are going away and what new ones should we be planning for? How does that impact our labor laws? How much worker monitoring and control will we give AI? Who is an employee and who is a contractor? What does the company need to do or provide to support the worker? Legislation is needed to untangle these changes. We know from experience that industrial revolutions aren't easy. We need to plan for and manage the changing nature of work. Most importantly we need to focus on creating new jobs, training and retraining people to adjust to new roles (Deming, 2020).

Disappearing Jobs

Routine work of all types is vanishing. In their book, The Second Machine Age, MIT researchers Erik Brynjolfsson and Andrew McAfee indicate that routine jobs in sales, bookkeeping and food prep will vanish quickly. Another study indicates that over half of all jobs in the U.S. will disappear in 20 years. Many more say that robots are moving forward, and human labor is in retreat. The drama is unfolding but not the way we might think. Up to 47% of all jobs could vanish by 2029. This number could be even higher and job losses could come even earlier. This will vary by occupation, but many jobs will disappear when machines get better at jobs than humans. Language translation, writing essays and research papers, writing top 40 songs and truck driving are all set to vanish in the next few years. If anything, predictions made by the gurus of AI tend to underestimate not overestimate obsolescence in the workplace. AI wasn't supposed to be able to beat humans at games like Go until 2027 yet it happened in 2015; Google's DeepMind won twelve years earlier than predicted (Ratner, 2017).

In 2019 a Japanese company, SoftBank, opened cell phone stores with "Pepper" a humanoid robot that is "cute, reliable and endearing." No sales associates. Pepper is equipped with sensors, a chest-mounted tablet for the customer to enter information and an anti-collision system. Most importantly, Pepper has emotions. Pepper is equipped with several things that allow it to recognize emotions in the customers. It can identify sadness, joy, anger and surprise and determine if a person is in a good mood or not. This makes Pepper a perfect personal assistant. And more than 10,000 Peppers are now at work at SoftBank, Pizza Hut, on cruise ships, and in homes and grocery stores. Pepper is no novelty. For many, this bot is a sign of "the robots are coming for your job."

If things were going the way many gurus predict, aggregate productivity would be going up, and jobs would be harder to find. But that's not exactly what is happening. As it turns out, productivity that measures how much the economy produces per hour of human labor is at a low point. Theoretically, if automation allows companies to produce more with fewer people, this number should be spiking. But it's not. It's lower than it's been since 1947. This is not what economist would expect to see if efficient robots were replacing efficient humans in mass.

Unemployment is low, and employers are complaining about a shortage of skilled labor, and therein lies the key to the mystery. Skilled vs unskilled labor accounts for the differences in supply and demand. Unskilled labor is being replaced and skilled labor is seeing shortages. Another phenomenon is happening to ramp up this drama and that is "job churn," which means people are moving from company to company and industry to industry.

Doomsday forecasters expected this to be very high when AI started to really infiltrate the job market. It turns out that it is much more nuanced and limited than predicted. It turns out that AI is leading to structural changes in the economy not just less and less jobs.

Unquestionably, manufacturing was one of the hardest hit sectors for job loss in the last twenty years. Robots came in and many, many manufacturing jobs were lost. Automation was not the only issue with the loss of these jobs. Politics and trade deficits also played a key role. Nevertheless, technologies have played and will continue to play a crucial role in defining jobs in years to come. This applies not only to how many jobs will exist in a field but what they look like and how they are performed.

As to self-driving cars and trucks, AI and machine learning is only beginning. Certainly, there will be a massive impact and that impact will unfold over years. Outsourcing work to machines is not new. Humans have been doing it for years from the washing machine to the dishwasher to the car. Again and again jobs are destroyed, and new ones are created. What is really important is how dreadful we have been at forecasting what those new jobs will be.

Fears about technologies are not new. Automation and computerization are not new. Humans are preprogramed to "fear the future." We are fretting about a robot dominated world but if that really does happen, GDP should grow, not stagnate. In other words, we should all be much better off. That is as long as we share the wealth (Surowiecki, 2017). On one hand, corporate executives act like they are concerned for workers because of automation. On the other, they simultaneously embrace innovative technologies. They have to in order to improve efficiency and remain competitive with others. The bottom line is that in a capitalist world it's all about making money. Capitalism is all about return on investment (ROI). There is a tremendous amount of pressure to increase revenue and drive profits. If a job can be done more cheaply and better by a computer than by a human being, then the computer will do it. Instead of reflecting on fear and anxiety, it's time for humans to plan for the jobs on the horizon.

This kind of revolution is different than the agricultural revolution or industrial revolution. This time humans are being challenged in the one area that has always made us unique, our ability to think. In the revolutions that came before, from hunter gatherer to farming, from farming to industrial, we didn't have to worry about thinking. Our intelligence is what differentiated us from everything else.

The impact this is having on the labor force is staggering. Incomes at Google and Facebook are in the mid six figures. The problem is not a shortage of STEM skills but a shortage of thinking skills. Knowing just doesn't cut it anymore. This new era spotlights deficiencies in our educational system. Our ability to teach people to think at higher levels needs improvement. These differences are magnified by differences in income and exposure to decision making and choices. Lower income children just don't have as much exposure to critical decision making. The gap between haves and have nots is getting wider (Ames, 2019).

All roads lead to employment. Every discussion of economic growth, equity and advancement comes back around to "will there be jobs that pay." AI and automation will enhance productivity, but will they help with income disparity? The effects will be more significant in some fields than others. Half of the jobs in the banking and insurance industries will disappear. The defense industry is certainly impacted. Finance and accounting, as well as healthcare, IT, engineering and government will be transformed. Easier jobs will get easier. Intellectually difficult jobs will increase. Re-education and consistent retraining will enable the agile workplace to change and grow. Learning will be a lifelong journey. In Finland, the Ministry of Economic Affairs and Employment stated that the minimum age for compulsory education should be 65 years of age. We will see gaps in competencies and imbalances in the labor markets. Companies are going to need to step up and provide ongoing education for everyone, not just leaders and the C-suite (Soininvaara, 2019).

AI and intelligent automation continue to disrupt everything. Many areas are being affected: customer care, call centers, document classification, production lines and factory floors. In all of these places humans are currently being replaced by smart robots and algorithms. AI can also eliminate bureaucracies and improve service for everyone. AI has proven very effective in handling monotonous tasks. It is pretty effective at handling even more complex operations like processing multiple signals, complex data streams and acting in real time. An example is autonomous vehicles that can sense the environment then respond and make decisions on the spot.

AI currently exists that can manage customer requests by understanding natural language. AI can resolve issues by estimating customer intent, processing large volumes of data and applying corporate policy. AI can suggest the best action on a particular case and communicate that back to the customer. And yes, AI can turn it over to a human anywhere along the way. That is if it understands that is needed. All this can happen in milliseconds as part of a voice or text conversation. It cuts out human customer service. It minimizes the need for human intervention. It creates a solution that makes the human team smaller and the AI more independent (Krasadakis, 2018).

AI will not only eliminate positions and disrupt companies, it will transform industries. One of the most prominent is the defense industry. Incorporating AI and robotics into traditional battle networks will improve current performance in the field and off. Since the end of the Cold War, the defense industry has been dominated by very large contractors. The question isn't whether AI and robotics will find their way in, the question is who will provide them. These organizations are large and built around legacy systems. The robotics driven revolution is a decade or so away, but smaller private sector firms are grabbing those defense contracts now. Over sixty percent of all AI and robotic contracts are issued to smaller private technical firms. In the past military technologies took years, even decades to develop. This is not how the new adaption cycle is moving. It is fast, very fast.

Every aspect of military operations, land, sea, air, space and cyber, is affected. Established contractors are underestimating the impact on their business. They are choosing not to compete in areas they don't feel comfortable. This phenomenon is known as "segment retreat." This is where a business chooses not to compete in an area that is new. The results can be seen from Blockbuster to Kodak. When organizations are large and not agile it is very hard to move beyond business as usual. This results in a downward spiral where organizations who don't adapt face disruption and decline. New players enter the fields and emerge to fill the gaps (Gons, E. et al, 2018).

Manufacturing is another industry that will be totally reformed. Many people believe that robots and AI will replace humans altogether and most jobs will be eliminated. This can be a sensitive subject and one that is intentionally ignored. AI is not going away. AI is evolving and companies that choose to keep up with new and emerging trends will quickly transform with it. AI is taking over routine decision making and speeding up daily operations and processes. AI is transforming the manufacturing ecosystem. It is influencing ERP (Enterprise Resource Planning), networked supply chains and predictive analytics. It is supplementing decision points, and eliminating routines and administrative tasks. It can manage workflows, create reports, reorder cycles and flag potential hazards. These types of automations can be huge time savers. They improve production and save money. In manufacturing, hands-free personal assistant bots can be very valuable for safety and inquiries.

By using facial recognition, AI can be used for security clearances. Facial recognition can also be used for quality control. The same technology that recognizes faces can determine if a product is in the correct packaging area. It can also investigate differences. It can help to eliminate fraud and flag atypical customer orders. Predictive analytics can be very valuable in supply chain management. AI can predict project demand and supply resources. All of this aids in establishing a component of AI called machine learning. This can streamline complex decision trees. It can assure that companies follow safety rules. AI use can include managing stock supplies and vendor selections.

The number of smart factories is increasing everywhere. Unemployment might be creeping into the unskilled labor force, but highly skilled AI technical workers are more in demand than ever. Another trend is to outsource automation and AI. Third parties are often used that support cloud-based operations. Many manufacturers use cloud-based operations. Often the experts that support the technology become the company's experts. Working with a third party also ensures current and up to date uses of the technologies. It offloads security and liability issues. It also helps with staying competitive and relevant, and modernizes how decisions are made (Castellina, N. 2018).

What You Know Won't Matter

Finance is another area adopting AI. Finance and accounting were always equated with crunching numbers. Finance departments do analysis to support accurate reporting and growth. Traditionally, this involved a lot of manual operations like creating spreadsheets and applying formulas to create statements and predictions. Automation and AI can increase reporting accuracy and efficiency exponentially. From invoicing to payments, to investments, AI can and is playing a role. The transformation to FinTech is irresistible. It frees the financial department up to focus on higher order thinking, like providing strategies and solutions. But how long will it be before AI replaces humans in that role too? It can make decisions faster, better and cheaper than humans in many situations. It's all about the data. Finance has a lot of "grey areas" that depend on professional expertise. The focus is shifting from crunching the numbers, which AI can do much better than humans, to analyzing the data, then applying it to relevant questions like "What does this mean for future investments?" or "How does this impact the competition?" Certainly, reporting can be done by AI in a more timely manner and at less expense (AVIDCHANGE, 2018).

Another group of professionals headed for possible obsolescence is doctors. AI has the potential to be more accurate at diagnoses, performing surgeries and keeping up to date with the current medical research. Machine learning is not subject to the same inherent biases that humans share. While relationships with patients is often the reason given for maintaining humans in the role of doctors, it is also the problem. Machines are capable of being much less biased than humans and don't have the same conflicts of interest. In some cases, interacting with a robot could eliminate patients feeling shame. In others, a correct diagnosis may be more important than empathy or continuity.

The main challenges today for healthcare is rising cost and insufficient number of doctors. AI can be cheaper than hiring new staff. It is also universally available and can monitor patients remotely. Currently, the reason used for maintaining doctors is human bonding and the compassion that is shared between doctor and patient. But how long will it be before computers can show emotions, devotion and concern? Many AI systems already do.

What about programmers and software engineers? Are these professions going to be impacted? In the short term, the next ten years, probably not significantly. In the longer term, most definitely. The game is changing. Programmers no longer always write the step-by-step instructions, but instead focus on instructing the computer to recognize situations and react to them. Engineering is going to be around a bit longer than most other professions. The caution is that most neural network operations are black boxes. In AI, a programmer acts like a coach. The capabilities of AI, machine learning and neural networking are wondrous, magnificent and here to stay. Automated reasoning and acquired knowledge are what makes AI… well… AI. Programmers, like so many other professions, are redesigning their jobs. AI engineers will still be needed to create tests and research AI applications. AI is only beginning to take hold, but once it does it will be with us for a long time. Engineers are the backbone of technology (BMJ, 2018).

AI, as it stands now, is categorized into two types of intelligence: general intelligence and specific intelligence. General intelligence is based on the theory that machines can be made to think like humans. Machines can have functions that are similar to the human brain, operating with understanding, compassion, reason and logic. When this happens programmers and software engineers will be obsolete. Specific AI refers to a computer's ability to perform specific tasks. AI performs these tasks much better than humans could do them. This is closer to where AI evolution is currently. In many ways and areas, AI is still in its infancy. For now, we will still need software programmers and engineers in areas like healthcare, manufacturing, transportation, food production, customer service, finance, defense and many others.

There used to be a paradigm that said if you work for the government, your job is safe for life. That, however, has changed. Even governments may become obsolete with AI. The private sector is implementing AI and intelligent solutions to problems many governments around the world are still unable to solve. Simple management, payroll, cataloging and financial systems are a legacy. The gap between the private and public sector's ability to reach and apply technologies is widening. As technology becomes more advanced and complex, it becomes more disruptive. Then there is the question of talent. Traditionally the private sector has and does pay better than the public sector. And a current crisis of trust is infiltrating governments all over the globe. As the workforce moves to digital and remote, there are more expectations on government to keep up with technology. Most of our governments are dated. There is a relevance gap reflected in outdated and inadequate services and slow-moving processes and procedures. As AI disruption infiltrates the workplace more people will begin to question why government is what it is. More importantly, why they are paying for it.

The labor force will change, and temporary work will increase. The public sector will need to change and adapt a more agile approach to structures and strategies. It won't be as simple as overlaying digital solutions onto current procedures and processes. From education to healthcare and civil service, the governments of the world will need to transform how they operate. Blockchain will take over screening, and eliminate countless agreements, contracts and reimbursements currently handled by clerks. The transformation of public institutions may very well be the biggest challenge of the twenty-first century. The slower they are to adapt and the more governments cling to "the way we have always done it," the less relevant public institutions will become.

Security is one area where a strong government presence is needed. Government needs to focus on risk and cybersecurity in all areas. Cybersecurity programs, legislation that addresses privacy concerns and the handling of data, are critical. It might be necessary to establish new units and look at new cost structures. It will definitely require an agile approach and reviewing and focusing on data. Legacy programs must remain workable, but upgrading is essential. Government must become competitive and willing to change processes that date back over half a century. The days of decade-long programs and solutions are gone. Moving forward, agile solutions and ongoing upgrades and improvements are what's critical (Johal, S. 2017).

Positions of the Future

Cognizant is doing a wonderful job of fortune telling our futures at work. In 2017 they came out with a white paper stating a positive approach to viewing AI in the workplace. It's about time. There is a lot of negative out there. Because AI is moving so fast, it can be scary. The article published in 2017 begins to imagine changes. What will new jobs based on AI's emergence in the workplace look like? One of the assumptions is that humans are going to be eliminated in the workplace, but the exact opposite is true. They will be more valuable than ever. To quote

Cognizant, "Humans have never been more integral to the future of work" (Cognizant, 2017). Their work is based on some simple principles: work has always changed, lots of current work is awful, machines need man, don't underestimate human imagination or ingenuity, technology will upgrade all aspects of society and technology both solves and creates problems.

In the 2017 paper they identify twenty-one jobs for the future and another twenty-one in the 2018 update. Even more can be found on their website. Will they all come to fruition? Who knows? What is important here is the focus on what AI can bring us and how we can redefine and retrain the workforce of the future. It will be very different. Organizations and industries will experience big changes. Some will survive. Others will recreate themselves and thrive. The key here is agility. Agile means alert, approachable, nimble, and quick to respond. Let's review some of the new job titles the future may hold: Data Detective, IT Facilitator, Ethical Sourcing Officer, AI Business Development Officer, AI Assisted Healthcare Technician, Cyber City Analyst, Financial Wellness Coach, Digital Tailor, Quantum Machine Learning Analyst, Virtual Store Sherpa, Augmented Reality Journey Builder, Flying Car Developer, Esports Arena Builder, VR Arcade Manager, Vertical Farm Consultant, Juvenile Cybercrime Rehabilitation Center Director, Algorithm Bias Auditor, Trust Officer and Smart Home Design Manager. These are just a few examples. (Cognizant, 2017, 2018).

What got us here won't get us there. Many people are excited and enthusiastic about what is emerging in the workplace. Others are scared that what little influence they had on the marketplace is disappearing quickly. One reflection is certain, humans want and need the human connection. Areas that support preparation, compassion and connection will flourish. The positions of the future will be what we make out of the new tools we have. This will take agility, innovative thinking and coaching. For entire industries to survive, they are going to have to reshape themselves; reinvent positions, products and markets; and retrain the workforce. Learning and development, adult education, traditional Higher Ed and even our K-12 systems are going to need to change how and why we educate. Humans are innovative, creative and always looking for a better way. They will eventually find it but the path ahead will not be straightforward or easy.

Even areas like auto repair accepted AI because insurance companies are pushing its adoption. In many industries AI is not a novelty, it's the norm. AI can help resolve claims more quickly and more accurately than humans. Remote estimates, using visuals, benefit policy holders and insurance companies (Marshall, 2021). But what about the auto mechanics doing the work?

There is no doubt the economy is being dislodged and disrupted but certain workers, young men and minorities in particular, are seeing the greatest displacement. Nonwhite and less economically secure workers are more likely to be replaced. People who lack education and people where significant differences exist across geographic and demographic areas are at risk. Food preparation, which is usually done by lower income, less educated, nonwhite workers, is likely to be 91% automated in the next five years. Ethnic minorities are often found in lower skilled jobs. Jobs that require reasoning, persuasion, laboring and politics are less likely to be disrupted. These patterns are not surprising considering men are the majority of workers in manufacturing and construction. Both of those industries will be impacted by automation and robots. The progress of AI will fall unevenly on the workplace. This is another reason why government at all levels, federal, state and local, needs to step up and help with re-skilling workers (Simonite, 2019). AI will make simple and repetitive tasks disappear first. As AI advances, any job that is redundant, even if it is more complex, will be at risk.

ASK THE HARD QUESTIONS

- Where will we see the effects of AI on unemployment in the next 10 years?
- How will we retrain workers for new jobs?
- What industries will be the most disrupted? Short term? Longer term?
- What positions will change and how? How will that affect you?
- How can we use AI to enhance work and not eliminate it?

Chapter 6

AI and Big Work-Life Changes

"It is not the strongest of the species that survive, nor the most intelligent, but the one most responsive to change."
—Charles Darwin

Both work and the workplace are starting to look very different. There's a disconnect. The pathways through hiring and education to career success are not keeping up with the workplace. Technology continues to advance. The line between soft and hard skills is vanishing. In 2019, University of South Florida did research and concluded that the six most important skills for the workplace in 2029 will be communications, problem solving, collaboration, ability to learn, creativity and resilience. All very human skills. What matters moving forward is not how difficult a skill is but whether that skill can be performed by machines.

Learning and education are needed throughout a worker's career to remain competitive and effective. We need a new way of looking at things. We need a bridge that makes the transition between learning and work seamless. Many Americans without a college degree are already unemployed. These people will feel the pain first. Low level jobs in retail, service and manufacturing have already disappeared. Going back to school is either too expensive, too inconvenient or irrelevant because, in many ways, the educational system is outdated. It was designed for a different time. Education has not been able to make the necessary changes for many reasons. The challenges of life are not any less significant. People are juggling families, work and other responsibilities. There is a tremendous need for innovation. We need to bridge the gap for underserved communities between learning and work (Strada Education Network, 2019).

Problem solving isn't going away for humans. We are still going to need thinkers, and leaders that can inspire, motivate and connect with others. There needs to be a change in focus away from humans as capital and toward a focus on human well-being. The traditional focus on capital spending and mission statements isn't enough. Humans should be the central focus of the organization. This means taking into consideration social, environmental, diversity, inequality and urgency concerns and empowering change. This means supporting change for the individual, the organization and the workplace. This problem hasn't been solved. If anything, it has intensified. Technologies are bringing disruption to the very fabric of the human experience. It's a tense time of change and resilience. Those that can reinvent themselves will survive and flourish. The rest will not.

From Profits to People

The importance of humans in the workplace is not fading away. It is growing more important every year. Employers will have to reinvent or perish. This is a big job because it isn't just window coating, it's redesigning how organizations think about people. It starts with human resources and the role it plays in organizations. Changing the focus from profits to people takes bravery. Employment has become precarious with more layoffs, short term contracts and new rules. Research supports the fact that the number one reason people leave their jobs is the lack of opportunity to learn and grow.

Human Resources (HR) has traditionally focused on administrative tasks, not making the organization money. HR is usually considered to be overhead. In many organizations HR has been fighting for a seat at the table for years. Robotic Process Automation (RPA) is changing that. RPA is capable of many of the manual tasks and rule-based and repetitive activities under HR. Many HR departments are using chatbots to do what people used to do. Chatbots have invaded the HR space and surveys show that there is a lot more RPA on the way.

There are various levels of sophistication with bots. Simple bots that just answer frequently asked questions have shown some success. They look for keywords and then match and provide "canned" previously determined responses. For example, a worker may ask the bot to describe benefit options for healthcare. The bot will respond with a list based on their job title. Intelligent bots try to respond with more dynamic responses. These are based on natural language matching. The bot may set you up with a benefits representative. This invasion is dynamic and moving into smaller companies and shared spaces quickly. These bots are trained on the company policies and procedures and can help with first-line services. They operate on first call resolution and self-service principles. Often these algorithms are very complex. Usually, they are unknown and secret to the organization. The more advanced the bot the more sophisticated the tasks.

Voice activated technologies like Google Home and Amazon's Alexa are finding their way into the workplace. Employees expect access to the same technologies at work they have at home. Organizations are interested in automating tasks and cutting costs. The benefits are plenty. They can improve productivity, quickly address issues, collect data, and foster allegiance and satisfaction. They free up HR people who have always had to do this transactional type of work to do other things, often more strategic and creative. It's not all negative. Chatbots can have a very positive impact on the workplace and the employee experience. They are still only in the stages of early adoption. Of course, there is another, darker side. These bots are listening.

Today's workers are digital consumers. They rely on technologies both at home and in the workplace. Their expectations are high. They are sick of using apps and apps are expensive to develop. Oftentimes employees have a difficult experience using apps. This creates a fragmented environment. Virtual assistants are an alternative. They can seamlessly integrate an otherwise fragmented experience. Transactional HR systems, with multiple applications, can be combined. Instant messaging is how people have learned to communicate. Virtual assistants allow workers to message. This is the same way they interact with each other outside of work (Attra, 2018). HR is using this technology for many reasons even more important than talking with employees. They are setting themselves up to be the leaders of change in the organization. Most organizations find change difficult. HR can use AI for open enrollment, payroll and taxes, scheduling, recruiting, promoting and feedback.

Can I Talk to a Human Please?

That's not all that's happening. The U.S. Army uses a chatbot for recruiting. Call centers use them to provide customer service suggestions. Others use them to allow workers to check their schedules. Other bots can arrange for employee time off or inform management about unexpected sick days or leave. In order to do this and do it well, a few criteria have to be in order. To begin with, the organization has to have a well-defined process. And they need data that is easily accessible to the bot. Oftentimes there is scripting and programming involved, and this requires customization. This is especially true with vocally activated systems. And then there is the problem of change. What if the laws change? Or the policy changes? Or the processes change? The bot will not change on its own.

This revolution is also displacing workers. Ultimately, the reason AI is finding its way in the workplace is the effect on the bottom line. AI reduces labor costs. AI can add real value and tangibles like providing employee service 24/7. But the bottom line is they don't call out sick, they don't need benefits and they don't leave and increase the turnover rate. They save money. In order to save money organizations are willing to reinvent themselves. Is it really that easy?

Change is coming to HR in another way. Traditionally, HR was in charge of the acquisition of talent. It probably still is in some organizations. HR is usually also in charge of learning and development as well as training. All aspects of performance measurement, from onboarding through performance reviews, falls to HR. The AI revolution is driving change in the way all this is done. Candidates are demanding more. Workplaces are requiring higher skills. Traditional education tracks just can't and don't keep up. Technologies are allowing learning to become more integrated with work. Learning is becoming more personal, and slowly it is shifting to lifelong learning. Inside expertise and talent mobility will drive more internal responsibility. Organizations can't expect to outsource and hire enough people with all the skills they need.

RPA (Robotic Process Automation) is springing up. It's being used for talent matching. Current employees and job openings are matched, across the enterprise, by skill-based algorithms. Internal mobility will be what makes a company sustainable in the age of AI. It cuts down on training, onboarding and rehiring. The more a company can hold on to and utilize the people who are already familiar with their systems, process and culture, the less time and money will need to be spent on getting productivity up to the expected level. Opportunities and training need to be extended to workers at all levels, not just those at the top.

The "Big Question" is are companies ready for this. It's a time of change. How we view learning, human experiences in the workplace, leadership, mobility, systems, rewards, teams and just about everything about the workplace is changing (Deloitte, 2019). Companies that can evolve and reinvent themselves will flourish. Others will perish. The future of our workplaces and our workforce will be very different than in the past. Organizations will focus on upgrading technologies and upskilling humans. HR will need to focus on effective learning and talent mobility. The more technology integrates our workplaces, the more focus we need to put on humans.

New Needs New Standards

COVID 19 opened the door to remote work. It was open before this but only on a small scale. The pandemic hit and within a year the flood gates opened. People started working remotely and realized they like it; companies realized they were saving money, big money. Some are still a little uncomfortable. Most are asking the question, "How can we make this better?" Gig, contract and freelance workers are accepted and strategic. This is especially true in highly technical fields. They come in many varieties. Gig workers are paid by the task and complete a specific piece of work. Freelancers are usually paid by the hour and hired based on time. There are many different titles for this type of work. What they are not is employees. Which means they are not covered, supported or restricted by standard 20th century employment benefits, laws, or policies and procedures.

It's time for new standards. Gig workers, freelancers and remote workers need support. They need support in their physical environment. They need support with training, health issues and accessibility. Very few states or national governments have committed to recognizing the role companies play in supporting this new workforce. Many organizations use these workers to process transactions, which makes them very vulnerable to change from AI. Very few organizations have adjusted to managing this workforce. They are used to "fill slots" and assimilate tasks not for strategic workforce solutions. It's short-term rather than long-term thinking. The real reason alternative workers are used is to enhance organizational performance. The new workforce requires a change in mindsets. The current message is "if your important we hire you."

The other thing this kind of labor force does is allow companies to experience is flexibility. If companies can move beyond short-term thinking, they can use this workforce strategically and deliberately. They can connect talent with the role and responsibilities. Companies need to make an investment. They need to expand the role HR plays in supporting the new workforce. This can range from ongoing recruiting, onboarding, learning and development to incentive pay and feedback. New platforms and technologies are quickly emerging to support this workforce. Technologies are not the sole solution to using and supporting alternative workers. It really comes down to a question of value and respect. Organizations that switch their mindset and take this workforce seriously will be well positioned. They will be able to engage talent and build strategies that adapt quickly to change (IBA Global, 2017).

AI has had several starts and stops along the road to successfully infiltrating the workplace. Some experts see this as evidence. Since AI can handle only minimal and narrow tasks, its impact on productivity will be marginal and slow. This of course relies on the old definition of productivity which is: more work done by fewer workers. Increased productivity then is defined as the same amount of work done by fewer workers. The worker is a widget and fewer of them cost less money. This might have worked in a prior era, but it won't hold up in the new workplace. Even the term "knowledge worker" coined by the infamous Peter Drucker in 1959 is obsolete. We are asking so much more than just knowledge from our workforce. AI is replacing and will continue to replace "knowledge." It will be much harder for AI to replace creativity, innovation and imagination.

Much of what happens now in AI is knowledge based. The education and health care industries are only two examples. Very few sectors of our economy will escape the impact of AI. Healthcare uses it to diagnose patients. AI prescribes treatments based on medical research and the probabilities of success. Similarly, Google and Chegg help students complete their homework. The transformation is already beginning. The data is available and being updated, and machine learning is growing. Algorithms are producing more algorithms. AI impacts everything from ads on your mobile phone to delivery at your doorstep. The data never stops flowing or growing.

The only thing slowing AI down is a lack of understanding of what is possible. AI is following the pattern of many earlier technologies. Tech firms and large companies are the leaders. Startups spring up as new ideas and new markets open up. Mid-sized businesses follow when the technologies become affordable and available. Big companies have the money to invest and the people to make AI happen. Smaller companies are interested in surviving, competing and staying alive. AI is likely to help big companies get bigger and make it harder for small companies to compete. Adopting AI is not easy for large organizations. AI has to be integrated with the current systems and processes.

Business processes evolve over time. Once they are established, they are very hard to change. Simple, isolated use cases are usually successful. Large-scale integrations that require major process modifications or adapting new processes entirely are a different story.

AI still requires humans to ask the questions and define what they want as results. It also requires someone to label data initially, then monitor and audit the results. The titles AI Auditor and Chief Trust Officer are turning up. Usually this requires highly skilled and expensive talent. This talent can be hard to find.

A perfect example of monitoring and auditing results is RPA and customer service. This sounds like it is simple and straightforward, and it can be for

RPA is Everywhere

smaller scenarios. On a larger scale, it can be very difficult. RPA requires the integration of existing systems and changes in processes and architectures over time. Much of what is out in the marketplace masquerading as AI is not. It is really decision driven, statistical machine learning. It uses labeled data and a set of user defined rules. Rule based systems are pretty easy to develop quickly and inexpensively. But the results are also limited. Just like with natural language recognition, it is the human side of the operation that makes it more challenging. Projects take longer and cost more than expected (Davenport, 2019).

AI has and will continue to impact the workplace in three important areas: automating tasks, analyzing data and engaging in conversations. This includes robots, RPA, chatbots, vocally activated technologies, intelligent agents and machine learning. AI is everywhere. Advice is cheap and AI is making it cheaper. Any industry that is data driven can use AI to become more valuable and less expensive.

Machine learning has given organizations the ability to create very specific and highly accurate classification and prediction models. This is one of the biggest strengths of machine learning. It builds statistical models that can instantly calculate and present results. It's like statistics on steroids. Machine learning can learn from data. Then it creates more highly effective models. From simple regression analysis to decision trees and randomization, machine learning can produce results quickly. It can help improve market analysis, pricing, and revenue management.

Pinpointing, targeting, identifying, modeling and developing recommendations is what RPA does best. Machine learning has transformed how we work by giving us the ability to analyze just about anything that comes from data. This gives us the illusion of making better, quicker, and more efficient and effective decisions. But are we really? Human decision makers are not always reliable. It's very likely that mid-level decisions like which products to sell this spring and who to assign to the project will be made by machines. Then there is the reality that it is easier for machines to deal with really big data (rivers, lakes and oceans) than it is for humans. There are a few challenges that only humans can discover. Is the data labeled? Is it available? Does it match the variable being predicted?

RPA is relatively cheap to implement. It performs easily structured, information intensive tasks. What makes a task RPA eligible? Repetition, and a sequence of structured tasks that can be identified in advance with some precision. RPA inputs and accesses one or more information systems. RPA is good for tasks where all contingencies can be identified. It works where human judgment and unpredictable interactions do not apply. More and more intelligent agents and chatbots are using a combination of RPA and machine learning and or natural language processing.

RPA is a good example of freeing up workers from repetitive tasks. They have the ability to do more work or give better service with the same number of workers. But RPA is not without challenges. A major issue is often the internal systems architecture, since RPA uses what the organization has and quite often these systems are challenging. Another issue is business processes often need to be redesigned. This can take a long time and a lot of effort. This depends on the agility of the organization, business, department or team.

That's Not All AI Can Do

OCR (Optical Character Recognition) is another way organizations are using AI. It is used to combine and analyze data. It's been around for decades. The cloud has made a huge difference in OCR. Different documents and communications are combined across multiple data sources. OCR uses them to analyze and assess business objectives. Speech recognition has also impacted how AI is used in the workplace. You can shop online using it on your computer or phone if the site has speech recognition. It works as long as the organization can structure the data. Currently AI agents are used for processes that deal with customers and customer information. AI can respond if the responses are straightforward, don't require empathy, understanding of emotions or complex interaction. Voice recognition and vocally activated technologies are growing. People can be impatient, and they expect the same conveniences in the workplace they have at home. "Alexa find a recipe for whipped cream icing for me."

Other areas of big change in the workplace brought on by AI are more global and far reaching. AI is having a fundamental impact on the global labor market and will continue to do so for many years. The impact on organizational structures, work time, labor relations and the working environment are emerging. AI is changing the world of work fundamentally. Organizational structures are being shaken at their foundations. The skills needed to succeed in the workplace are changing. The structures and processes of the organization are changing. Everything is changing.

AI is forcing us to look at the global workplace. Global institutions are moving toward strategic approaches to human resources. AI will have a fundamental impact on workers. Blue collar and white-collar workers will be affected. The more single steps in the working process can be described the sooner employees will be replaced by intelligent algorithms. How this "fourth industrial revolution" will unfold depends on the technology development within each country. It depends on the skills of the young people who will shape the next labor force. Developing countries like India and China lack social security systems and other infrastructure that help people who lose their jobs. In the end, jobs with low or medium requirements will be eliminated. The prediction and percentages vary. What is important is a high number of low skilled people could be unemployed in countries that are neither rich enough nor well prepared enough to have a safety net in place (IBA Global, 2017).

Creativity and flexibility will become more important. Education will only be relevant as it relates to the task. For example, much of the work of an accountant can be done by an intelligent algorithm. The expectations for what people do will be much higher. Making the necessary investment now will pay off in the future. Systems will need to be connected. We need to open intelligent communication channels. Employees will have to get used to the new technologies. Retraining will be continuous while the restructuring of the jobs and the workplace unfolds. There will be implications for unions, legislatures and collective bargaining. Anything that affects the position of human beings within the world of work is subject to change.

Organizations will feel the impact on their internal and external processes. Anything that is routine, whether it is physical or cognitive, will be impacted. Internal reorganization and then the ability to do it again will be vital for survival. The traditional pyramid structure within organizations will not support this well. Hierarchies are not usually flexible.

The individual's workplace will also change. Each individual will become more autonomous. Intelligent assistants will perform many of the daily routine tasks now performed by employees.

Workers will need to know how to communicate with these intelligent systems and robots and this will require training. COVID catapulted many into the remote workplace. It was only the beginning. Employees don't have to be in the same place at the same time in order to exchange information. Technology has changed all that. Those companies that don't have structures and systems flexible and integrated enough to support an autonomous workforce will need to upgrade. Those that do will need to refine processes and work on communication channels.

Companies will begin to cross borders and open up boundaries. Structures referred to as matrix structures allow for technical supervision and disciplinary supervision to be treated separately. Generally technical instruction comes from an individual employee by another organization. Activities in the matrix structure cross borders and so does supervision. Standards can be used and enforced across organizations and even countries. In the future international labor agreements may become standard in some sectors.

Imagination, Curiosity and Empathy

We can look forward to sharing space with all kinds of robots. Workers will work next to robots that support them both with physical labor and cognitive tasks. As companies roll out intelligent systems and integrate them into the workspaces, there will be a strong need for employees to be well trained in technical skills. This is important not only for operations but also for employee safety (IBA Global, 2017).

In the past employers created a stable job role that had a written description. Jobs will shift from predictable to interpretive. The new job skills will be more about listening, creativity and responding, not about meeting any written structured requirements. New "super jobs" will have titles like analyst, manager, director, designer and architect. This is going to require so much more than just rewriting job descriptions. It will require supporting human skills like imagination, curiosity and empathy.

The narrow view of skills, activities and tasks just won't cut it without highly specific roles. Organizations will need to broaden their perspectives. They will need to open up their level of trust to support human communications and ingenuity. Job descriptions will need to look at results, outputs and problems solved. Terms like supervise and manage will be replaced by motivate and engage. Learning and development will be a daily activity in the regular flow of work. This will often happen in real time. Organizations will be challenged to reimagine work.

Ready or not here it comes! New technologies are impacting everything we do. They will determine the long-term success (or not) of companies in almost all sectors of the global economy. There will be new business models and more new technologies. Organizations will have to change current best practices and create new ways to operate. At the core of this is the belief that they can change. HR and L&D (Learning and Development) are essential to this transformation. In order to move the needle on business performance there will be a need for constant training. Companies will need to create a new learning centered culture. Technology is to improve human lives and organizations. Too often organizations focus on the features of that technology and not on how the technology is implemented. The focus needs to be on the solution not on the technology. It doesn't matter if it is AI, IOT or a simulator, the technologies are here to improve human performance.

ASK THE HARD QUESTIONS

- Should humans let robots make decisions?
- Should the military let robots make the decision to kill?
- How will we support humans that do not work?
- Do we use robots in production processes that require complicated technical steps in the middle of a process flow?
- Can computers be programmed to really innovate and do creative research?
- What risks do these new technologies have on your workplace?

Chapter 7

Agile Transformation

> "Learn from yesterday, live for today, hope for tomorrow. The important thing is not to stop questioning."
> —Albert Einstein

AI and Agile business processes go hand in hand. AI holds the key to opening the door for both flexible business processes and continual delivery. Agile started as a way to keep software projects moving forward. It has found its way into the very fabric of organizations. Agile, like AI, can affect everything in the workplace. It affects procedures from budgeting, to staffing and production metrics. It affects how teams from different areas work together (for example: marketing, production and technology). Leadership has to understand it, back it and not be afraid to move it forward. It's a moving target. In this way, it's just like AI.

Organizational culture generally falls under HR. What really happens in companies is a combination of mergers, acquisitions, retention, compulsions, recruiting issues, and ideas from whomever is in charge. Large companies are a mix of cultural, political, operational, physical and technical structures coming together over time. Agile is a mindset and a leadership style. The foundation of Agile is the Agile Manifesto. Agile project management became popular because of the digital transformation. It is not the same as the dictionary definitions common for the English adjective "agile." Agile is about doing as opposed to being paralyzed by over planning. In Agile you get the minimal necessary requirements and start working.

The four core values of Agile software development as stated by the Agile Manifesto are:

- individuals and interactions over processes and tools
- working software over comprehensive documentation
- customer collaboration over contract negotiation; and
- responding to change over following a plan

Agile needs an organization that is flexible and able to move and change. It needs an organization that puts people first not processes and procedures. And it needs an organization with the vision to see into the future. So does AI. AI will require more than Agile teams; it will require Agile architecture. Most organizational structures, especially larger global organizations, are not responsive by design. They struggle with integrating things that are new. They attempt to improve effectiveness with new buildings, new testing and new people. Change is frustratingly slow. To the people that work in these kinds of organizations, whatever the industry, rapid change seems like a mirage. Successful business objectives mean an annual review with HR that is for the most part meaningless unless it includes a raise.

Agile is key to integrating AI with compassion and empathy. AI represents the blending and blurring of human and technology capabilities. AI will bring tactical and strategic changes to how entire industries operate. Changes like deep learning will cross channels and boundaries. These changes will open up new ways of thinking and operating. The more AI brings into focus the more changes will impact existing processes, procedures, systems, products and people.

What If AI Isn't for Us?

AI has built very large organizations, quickly. The major assets for world changing innovation are ideas and code. The boundaries between human interactions and AI are constantly moving forward. With the pervasiveness of AI everywhere across the globe, you may have no choice but to use AI. It might be a matter of surviving. Organizations will be challenged to change their mindsets, their processes and often their products. Those that can rethink, reengineer and retrain with an interest in humans over profits will have the greatest chance of surviving.

There is no magic pill for changing company culture. It can't be changed by edit and it usually evolves over time. Some organizations are about control and competence. Others are about collaboration and cultivation. It depends on how they view and value people. Organizations that are collaborative usually provide more feedback and less judgment. There's a higher degree of trust and less fear of failure. New ideas are welcomed, and failure isn't fatal. The idea of maximizing value requires an interactive rather than a linear or top-down approach. This is where AI enters the picture. AI is there to provide the data, the analytics and the information quickly as well as improve process flow and production.

AI should be positioned to improve results not to eliminate activities. Results are outcomes. They happen at the end of a series of activities. Outcomes can be subdivided, and then subdivided again and again. Achieving objectives is the sum of many series of activities at many levels. Outcome orientation allows people to act with autonomy. It is a place where people are trusted and can achieve results. This requires bringing down the silos. It requires having conversations. Humans talking and sharing. Agile transformation starts with valuing input from people. Agile gives people a sense of purpose and value. They can see how their efforts contribute to outcomes.

Agile organizations aren't centralized or decentralized. It is about architectures that solve the problems now. These may change in the future. It is not a one-way street. Business structures can and probably will have to change and change again. AI will be integrated into different activities leading to new processes and outcomes. AI will find its way into businesses to replace activities and improve outcomes. It's very important that organizations evaluate what outcomes are important, and then ask how AI technologies can and will help to improve them, always monitoring and auditing the impact of AI on business outcomes.

AI is About Continuous Improvement

AI is about continuous improvement not just in the technology itself but how it serves an organization. No industry is immune to the impact of AI now or in the future. AI will become more and more important to the operations of most organizations. An organization should have a goal in mind with AI integration and then monitor results. This will require more than just quantitative metrics. It is important to include qualitative value-oriented measures as well. Agile transformation requires engagement with those who are impacted by changes in the processes. The transformation to an Agile organization doesn't come from the top down. It involves feedback and monitoring just like successful AI integration.

How businesses are valued and what it means to be successful is changing. Calculating worth was a very tangible and measurable progression. Then the world changed. The most valuable companies in the world don't have large scale machines or wealth underground. Instead, they have people and code. These businesses have mostly invisible assets that are subject to change. From business objectives to continuous improvement, the Agile transformation infiltrated entire organizations. Based on more technologies coming our way very quickly, companies are being asked to rethink, restructure and reengineer everything.

Currently, AI application is limited. It supplements or eliminates an activity. It replaces a task or provides a niche service. But it won't be long until this progresses beyond the activity level. The magnitude will be much larger. Leadership with be critical in the Agile transformation. Leadership will need to set expectations, define outcomes and provide feedback. All this is critical to interactive performance. AI will find the way into many different areas. AI transformation will not happen without innate challenges. Many organizations will not be able to meet the demands of new technologies. From the beginning, companies need to ask "Why are we integrating these technologies? How will we measure success?"

For many organizations, transitioning to Agile and managing change takes a big effort. Many technologies will be replaced to incorporate AI. Many processes will be changed. People will have to be trained and retrained and then trained again. The term lifelong learning will take on a new meaning. Frequently companies just focus on new technology. AI will require most of the change to center on culture and organizational management. Technology will play a very small role in the AI transformation. The focus isn't and shouldn't be on the technologies. Instead, the focus should be on breakthroughs that AI is expected to help the organization achieve. All this will need to be tempered by an awareness of and empathy for the organization itself and the capacity to change. This is where humans come in and can add knowledge, expertise and insight. It's not a question of doing. It's more a question of AI forcing organizations to be Agile: to put people first, to have defined outcomes, to collaborate with each other and to be ready to respond to changes while following a plan (Deloitte, 2019).

Agile organizations come together to achieve outcomes and are organized around results. What does it take to own an outcome? It takes buying into the vision. It takes putting a plan and the talent together to make it happen. When organizations are departmentalized in the traditional way, each silo has its own priorities, and each function is a handoff. This takes up time. It slows everything down. Agile organizations are about organizing around outcomes not functions or specialties. This is where the term "DevOps" (Development Operations) comes into play. DevOps is the union of cross functional teams organized around outcome delivery. DevOps is people, process and technology coming together to add value. Setting up new structures in traditionally controlled organizations can take time and some effort. When it comes to change, these efforts will pay off (Gruver and Mouser, 2015).

Structures and Outcomes

Developing an accurate picture of the current structure will also help in revamping it. How high is it? How deep? Whether it is a pyramid or a matrix model or somewhere in the middle, the more top down or sideways layers the more difficult it is to move. Power struggles can easily emerge from authority and accountability. The results are anything but effective and agile. Agile is about movement, adjustment, fluidity, and awareness. When change comes quickly, the tradeoffs between costs and responsiveness are critical. Agile is crucial for survival.

Agile organizations ask, "What can we do to make that happen?" Change is not about predictability. It is not about "How much will that cost and how long will that take?" It is about response and accountability. "What can we make happen?" "How can we get that done by the end of the month?" Continuous delivery and analytics play a very important part in Agile transformation. This process helps to justify itself. "Fast Feedback and Fail Fast" are two sayings that follow this approach. With "AI" knocking at the door, some variety of the build-measure-learn loop so familiar to lean startups is key to Agile. Part of the building process has to include building the skills of human beings.

Many new systems claim to be AI. It's a broad definition. Some offer cost reduction or productivity and service improvement. HR systems for recruiting and talent matching are prime examples. Customer service apps are another key example. AI in its current state is more suited to operational work than asset creation. It can aid in asset creation in some areas. Design, develop, experience, deploy and test are usually not redundant tasks. Operational tasks like monitoring, maintaining and automating are more predictable. Sometimes these cross paths. When they do, AI can take over part of the operation as long as it is monitored and audited.

Budgeting and performance are areas to consider when organizations are looking at moving to Agile models. Annual reviews are limited. Monthly or quarterly reviews in both areas are much more beneficial. Updating as the year unfolds works much better than a calendar orientation. This allows for regular updates and better projections, which is needed for fluid and Agile transformations. Planning and feedback need to go hand in hand. There is no sense having monthly or quarterly performance reviews if the workers have not received feedback in that time period. Both feedback cycles and planning cycles have to be short term. Feedback has to be shorter than planning.

To be agile means to talk, discuss and collaborate often. Agile organizations need to focus on the worker and what they need to know next, not where they are now. Words like transparency and open access are important for agility. Traditional organizations share information on a need-to-know basis. This keeps people in the dark. Training is on an as needed basis. Certainly, some organizations will have information that needs to be restricted, and that's fine. Restrict on an as needed basis but keep the rest of the conversation open. Some industries are more controlled than others. This will have an influence on their ability to be agile. Some will be hit hard by the Agile transformation because of restricted industry controls. Others will find a way to keep under locks what is confidential and still open up to collaboration and sharing. The more information is open, the easier it is to move quickly.

With AI, the best fit is always better than the best tool. Implementation over operational features is critical. Implementation can take repositioning and training. It is not a one-time thing. A representative team of those intricately effected by the new technology needs to evaluate it. The teams determine the results. Then they map that back to the intention and objectives for installing AI in the first place. Does it fit the existing process? Does the business process need some improvement? The simpler and more straightforward the process, the easier it will adapt to and benefit from AI. Business needs to focus their efforts on what is under control. What can be contained in the features of the AI tool? And how does it align to business objectives?

ROI is Out and Rapid Change is In

When implementing any technology, especially AI, be careful with the metrics for measuring success. ROI, the popular metric for return on investment, often only tells part of the story. It is often not feasible to use ROI for training and certainly not for implementing rapid change. Peter Drucker's "If you can't measure it, you can't manage it" was a great saying for a very different era. Rapid change with new technologies requires not just measurement but forecasting. Who will be replaced? How will the process change? What training and upskilling are needed? Oftentimes there are many unknowns that are unknown. Rapid change has many unknowns. It is impossible to measure things you don't know about. What you can do is create an environment that supports the flexibility to adapt. You can change to a new variable once it becomes known instead of staying stuck in patterns that just don't work now. in an Agile organization, creating metrics that are adaptable to change is more important than predicting the future. The future is subject to change and to measures that are still unknown.

Change requires challenging the normal state of things. What's normal when things are changing rapidly? Having "AI" perform workplace functions instead of or in conjunction with humans is not normal yet. It's all new, and it's all happening quickly. Normal is what culture is all about. "This is how it's done here" or "This is the way we do it." Normal is the unstated reality that underlies a collective understanding of the way things are. Norms are culture and they affect workers' behaviors. Normal is what leads (or doesn't lead) to results. Cooperation as a norm is more consistent than competition, where there is a winner and a loser. Cooperation is what an organization needs to foster resiliency. This is key to adapting quickly to change. The more flexible and adaptable policies are, the quicker they are able to adapt (Narayan, 2015).

AI is about agile intelligence for business solutions. It is challenging. There is a need to understand the business requirements, the format and weakness of data sources and the existing systems. There is a requirement to understand the needs of the people who will use the information. It requires building an analytical data warehouse. Most of the time this warehouse will be fed from a variety of systems. The business will play a role in creating the data. AI requires a service-oriented design for collection and distribution of information. An agile transformation for business intelligence is about small pieces, small teams, small products, and alignment with big picture objectives. Performance metrics come from overall objectives. They align with key processes necessary to achieve those objectives.

And they align with the necessary organizational resources. How AI affects business intelligence depends on the service orientation.

Agile transformation is both a short term and a long-term effort. Let's compare an agile workplace to a sports team. While the game is going on, the team has to sense what is happening, adjust and act appropriately. After the game is over, it might be time to rewrite the rules. Similarly, for an organization to be Agile, it has to continuously rewrite the rules. They need to be flexible enough to allow for reactions in certain situations. Business processes that are fixed are not appropriate for knowledge intensive work, which is what AI is all about. Knowledge intensive services and support are dynamic but are not without problems.

Generally, business processes are anything but flexible. Change is the exception not the rule. When there are unforeseeable issues or high variability they don't respond well. Change is the exception to fixed business processes.. This is why collaboration is part of an agile transformation. Sharing information about tasks allows the data source to evolve. A "task" is a skill or a particular item that specifies the requirements and objectives of this work. Agile is about flexible adaption in a dynamic work environment. The more unique each task is the more difficult it is to use AI as a solution (Brander et al., 2011).

Agile can be described by a collection of practices. Practices like JIT (Just in Time), TQM (Total Quality Management), and people orientation are agile. Constant improvement, information sharing, transparency, and alliances are agile. Wide and deep skills training, motivation, and concurrent teams are agile. Worker support and openness are agile. Information is part of the agile operation. Integrating everyday practices like sharing information allows for new technologies to align with strategic objectives.

In many industries that rely on supply chain management, AI has already made its presence known. Old line manufacturing has integrated AI into the supply chain. This is in order to compete and survive. Intelligent agents manage the supply chain for one or more activities. Management coordinates these functions. Agile in these operation takes on the meaning of both flexibility and reconfigurability. Flexibility is an organization's ability to adjust processes according to the market, staffing and customer needs. Reconfigurability is the ability to adjust to changing demand (Lou et al. 2003).

Intelligent agents, forms of AI (or at least data analysis and machine learning), have three characteristics: autonomy, adaption and cooperation. Autonomy means they have a goal. They focus on that goal. They have an agenda. They conduct themselves in a manner to meet that agenda. They exhibit goal directed behaviors. They don't only react; they are proactive and can make decisions on their own when appropriate. Adaption means they take in information from the environment. They are constantly trying to improve. Cooperation means they share information with humans and other systems and agents. Multiagent systems (MAS) allow AI to work in an open and dynamic environment. Because machines can share information and perform coordinated functions much more quickly than humans, they are ideal for coordinating change (Mircea & Andreescu, 2011).

Agile doesn't mean no planning. Agile doesn't mean organizations can use it as an excuse not to prepare for change. The term "agile" has spread far beyond manufacturing and software development. Agile made its way into budgeting, human resources and family life. It's a powerful process but it is not an excuse to avoid planning and preparation. This is especially true with AI integration. It's still important to keep in mind what problems the introduction of AI is trying to solve and what problems it might create and then measure and monitor. The idea that quicker is always better isn't true. Especially when organizations are going into new areas and training on new frontiers. Keeping the end in mind and proceeding thoughtfully might be a better approach to integrating AI than moving fast and failing. Many times, long term data will reveal what short term analysis just cannot. The fundamental risk of integrating AI and not having a plan is that of moving too far too fast.

Agile puts the emphasis on prototyping and getting fast feedback. The organization goes with the skills they currently have both cognitively and physically and they accept the constraints. This automatically limits understanding and monitoring. They look for short term gains and never look at long term impact. For example: AI recruiting software may save a few dollars in employees reviewing resumes. It may narrow down the pool of applicants quickly. But what happens to those people once the company hires them? Do they become valuable employees? Do they stay? Sometimes without thought and planning the gains from AI can be short-term and short-sighted. The new technology is not sustainable or supportive of the company's long-term goals.

What can be even more frightening is that once the systems are in place, they stay there. The management team tells themselves that it is getting better. Eventually this will really work well. The future never materializes. No one is looking at the bigger picture. No one is stepping back far enough or long enough to realize the long-term effect of implementation on the organization. The technology is running the company rather than the company running the technology. Speed isn't everything in managing big change. Putting new intelligent systems in place is not necessarily making progress.

Most change in operations comes about incrementally. Incrementally doesn't mean it's not worth trying or it's not going to happen. Rather it means small steps that are monitored and reviewed carefully can and do bring about positive change. Agile is great once organizations have done the homework and as long as they continue to keep doing the work. It's not a one and done thing. What Agile can help organizations avoid is getting so bogged down the entire project gets derailed or sidelined and nothing happens. Agile is best when it is combined with thought and planning about what those final deliverables are and how to measure success. Implementing AI responds best to working backwards or backward solution design. Defining the end result and then developing ways to know you are reaching it in both formative and summative ways keeps things on track and forces organizations to monitor the impact along the way.

ASK THE HARD QUESTIONS

- How Agile is your organization?
- Do they value people really? Share information?
- Is your organization siloed? How quickly can things happen?
- What processes and procedures could be more Agile?
- Is technology running your company or are you running the technology?

Chapter 8

AI and Education Reborn

"If we do not change the way we teach, thirty years from now [2018] we will be in trouble."
—Jack Ma

AI will have enormous impacts on education, learning and talent development. In K-12, Higher Education and workplace learning, AI has barely scratched the surface. AI in education comes with opportunities and many challenges. AI technologies are being adopted at an unprecedented rate. AI will provide learner support. AI can interpret data. It can examine the role of the teacher or expert and AI can provide one-on-one tutoring. AI will provide us with insights on learning. It will measure innate characteristics like curiosity and creativity. AI will boost creative and higher-level learning. New pedagogies and research will be needed to take advantage of AI. AI is unquestionably going to have a very significant impact on how and what we learn. Humans will be increasingly working next to and with very smart machines.

AIEd (Artificial Intelligence in Education) is a broad topic. AIEd is finally picking up steam. It has been researched for over 30 years. Only recently has it been coupled with an understanding of what AI really is, what it can deliver and how it does what it does. Many simple versions of AI applications are already used in schools and HR departments. EDM (Educational Data Mining) makes predictions about your success or failure in the classroom or workplace. AIEd is not smart technology that adapts to what is liked rather than what is learned. It is not smart administration without more efficient learning. AIEd is smart technology that impacts the learning of every learner. It supports the teaching and training professions.

AIEd is in the very early stages. It needs to be further developed to allow for better learning experiences. Incorporating learning science is an integral part of the advancement of AIEd. It offers the possibility of learning that is more personalized, flexible, engaging and inclusive. It has the possibility of closing achievement gaps. It can help to increase teacher retention and development. It can help us learn how people learn.

Our educational system will need to perform at a higher level than in the past. AIEd investigates learning wherever it occurs. Learning happens in classrooms, workplaces, and really anywhere. This requires knowledge about the world. Data and algorithms are represented in AIEd models. These models include pedagogy, domains, and learners. Adaptive tutors (AT) are an example of combining all three models. They are adaptive and learn by continuous analysis. They use learner interactions, provide feedback and improve pedagogy. They use domains to provide efficient personal and context-based support.

AIEd has the power to address social, emotional and meta-cognitive aspects of learning.

Intelligent Tutoring Systems (ITS) simulate one-on-one human tutoring. Some even put the learner in control. Newer tutors use larger data sets. They are based on neural networks and on decision-making. This can limit and channel the information provided to the learner. This approach is challenged for a host of reasons. IAT (Intelligent Adaptive Tutors) models are far more flexible. They use learners' cognitive states, dialogue, semantics and natural language. IAT uses meta-cognition, scaffolding and social and emotional norms. These models measure the strengths of subconscious associations. They use mental images in memory (Luckin, et al., 2016).

K-12 is Broken

The K-12 education system served the United States well for over two hundred years. Who invented K-12 education? Horace Mann is given credit for our modern school systems. He was Secretary of the State Board of Education for Massachusetts. Horace developed a standardized curriculum. He believed it was important to educate all citizens. Mann's six tenets include: (1) Citizens cannot be both free and ignorant, (2) The public needs to pay for, maintain, and control education, (3) Children from all classes should have the same schooling, (4) Education needs to be non-secular (meaning not religious), (5) Education needs to use the principles of free society, (6) The educators and teachers need to be professionally trained. It was Mann who set up division by age (grades). He thought the lecture was the best way to teach. He built schools and reformed schools in Massachusetts. Other states adopted his approach. In over 200 years not a lot has changed (Broome, 2018).

The K-12 education systems have evolved in a variety of formats. They can differ greatly in graduation requirements. K-12 usually starts in preschool and runs through 12th grade (ages 3-18). States and local school districts decide the curriculum. They define the requirements for credits and funding. There is no final exam for graduation in the United States. This is unlike what exists in many other countries. There is a GED exam (General Education Development or Diploma). This can be a substitute for the normal graduation path. In order to attended post-secondary education, high school graduation or passing the GED is usually required.

Standardized tests, theoretically, were developed to measure aptitude and knowledge. The SATs were created in 1926 and the ACTs in 1959.

For over two hundred years, the K-12 system has provided institutions that serve three important purposes. They provide custodial care. They are community and social organizations. And they educate children. Most of the funding comes from the state (80%). Some support comes from the federal government and local governments (about 15% and 5%, but this can vary widely). The K-12 education system is usually divided into local school districts. It is managed by a school board. It heavily relies on real estate taxes. This results in huge disparity for education policies, needs, programs and curriculum. It always depends on where the school is located. The model of K-12 is time and place sensitive. It was developed to standardize education, not individualize it. It took care of children during the day when parents went to work on the farms and in the factories (Corsi-Bunker, 2006).

Technologies have found their way into K-12 education, but it has not been an easy few decades. Children 2 to 7 spend an average of two to five hours a day looking at screens (Welsh, 2018). Where children focus and their expectations have changed. The inclusion of technologies in K-12 education is backed by some of the biggest tech companies. The Gates Foundation, Amazon Web Services and Google support it. But it is still lagging. This is a generation ready to learn, that has grown up with technology as part of their life.

The five big obstacles to including technologies in K-12 are:

1. scaling and sustaining innovation
2. data privacy and ownership
3. evolution of teaching and learning
4. learning pedagogy
5. technology gap and digital equity

The five big reasons technology will influence K-12 education are: learners as creators, data driven practices, personalization, social and emotional learning and building capacity as leaders (COSN, 2019). This is where AI enters the picture.

Higher Education a Slippery Slope

Higher Education in many ways is more provincial than K-12. We can trace the history of Higher Education back to the University of Bologna in 1088. The establishment of European universities started with Oxford in 1100. It went to the Harvard model in 1663 and not a lot has changed. Most schools in the United States operate on some version of the Harvard model for Higher Education. This model is exclusionary by nature. It sets up a classic curriculum and prescribed course of study. It also sets up joint governance and faculty rule. This was followed by the Colonial Nine, which morphed into the Ivy League of today.

Expansion began after the Civil War with the creation of MIT (Massachusetts Institute of Technology). Later it included land grant and community colleges. Liberal arts, vocational and correspondence degrees became part of Higher Education. When the DOE (Department of Education) was established in 1886, about 5% of the population took part. Accreditation came late to Higher Education. Higher Education expanded again after World War II with the GI Bill of 1944 (Baggio, 2017).

Unfortunately, what has exploded in Higher Education is debt. This has created a very slippery slope for Higher Education. Many people are starting to question the value of a college education. Rising debt from school loans has certainly had an effect on the economy. Adjusted for today's dollars, the average cost of a college education in 1975 was $9,874 for private school and $2,336 for public institutions. In 2012 private institutions cost $28,989, and public $8,816. Personal income adjusted for 2012 dollars was $33,904 compared to real income in 1975 which was $34,352. The cost of higher education had more than tripled but real income was about the same. With higher costs came accountability. People began to ask is Higher Education worth it (Procon, 2019)?

In 1995, technology began to change everything. Online Higher Education was able to take space and time out of the equation. A host of online for-profit schools popped up. Some were good. Some were not so good. Gradually this would also impact more traditional schools. Tenure and the Carnegie hour slowed online adaption in many institutions. Gradually, LMSs (Learning Management Systems) and synchronous platforms found their way into the classroom. Why? Students were demanding it. In 2011 the world went to 4g and video, social media and webinars took off. This generation of college students grew up with technologies. More important was where they looked for knowledge. Knowledge had shifted from the classroom to the Internet. Higher education was being challenged by increasing economic weight. Schools everywhere began to compete for enrollment.

David Gelernter of Yale University stated in the Wall Street Journal, January 23, 2017, "Over 90% of U.S. colleges will be gone within the next generation, as the higher-education world inevitably flips over and sinks." Clayton Christensen stated much the same thing. He predicted in 2017 that half of the colleges could close in a decade. A degree from Harvard Business School costs approximately $400,000. The entire model of when and where we educate has changed. Young people are turning to corporations for learning and development. As Christensen said: "Let the students learn when they're ready and how they want to learn, not when and how we're ready to teach them" (Lederman, 2017). These two gurus are not alone.

Many Higher Education institutions are talking about faculty layoffs. They are downsizing to cut costs and stay alive. Much of what is called Higher Education is based on subject expertise. Expertise that surrounds a body of knowledge. Much of it redundant and repetitive. Intelligent systems are more than capable of presenting this kind of knowledge. Most learners have grown up with technologies. They expect it as part of the learning experience. There is a movement away from education for education's sake. Education now must have direct ties to the workplace.

The future of Higher Education is under great pressure. It will respond to upheaval by adapting new directions. It will be part of the new Agile workplace. Employees must always be ready to learn new skills. The challenge for Higher Education and a key to survival is to teach students workplace skills that AI can't replace. These skills are reliability, time management, social interactions, communication and accepting criticism. AI is currently widely used for homework. It will take over redundant and repetitive knowledge. Blended, online and mobile learning will be driven by user demand, preference and economic restraints (Tulinayo, et al., 2018).

Check the Box Learning

For a long time, workplace learning was about compliance and checking the box. Nearly 85% of corporate training was done in the classroom. It was systems or compliance based. The movement toward PoW (Point of Work) training has accelerated. In 2020, about 60% of workers have a chatbot, vocally activated voice assistant or robot in the workplace. Nearly 47% of customers have some form of AI for customer service. Economics implies that more industries are using some form of AI to automate business processes. Businesses are rushing to use AI for customer service, lead generation, client engagement, messaging communication, human resources, etc. Although the current AI is far from perfect, it will improve over time.

Business need is expanding the use of AI. AI is changing workplace learning. Linked directly to the Internet of Things (IoT), AI is triggered by observations and transactions. Collaborative systems are on the horizon. They are approaching quickly. Workplace economics and technology are converging. This will spark huge changes in the field of learning and development. Research suggests that nearly 45% of the activities performed in the workplace can be automated (Baggio & Omana, 2019).

The expectations of the older and younger generations in the workplace are very different. The older generation is more likely to expect training courses, at a certain time, in a certain place. Younger generations have different attention spans, expect micro videos and JIT (Just in Time) learning. They expect mobile, relevant and on demand experiences. Training in the past was done only as needed. It was scheduled and limited. Workers will demand training when they want it. The concept of learn to work will be transformed into work to learn. Training will not be proprietary.

The movement is away from generalized learning to individual learning. Learning will also be continuous and ongoing. Why? The workplace is changing rapidly. Workers must constantly acquire new skills. Many industries are at risk. Information is everywhere. The ability to apply information to solve business problems and meet objectives is what is needed. Kirkpatrick's Four Levels of Evaluation will become irrelevant. Everything will start at level 3. Can it be applied? The future of workplace training is with AI. Artificial intelligence will provide data-driven advice based on worker performance and needed skills (Jenkins, 2019).

Learning to Think

AIEd brings AI into the learning environment. It uses AI to represent knowledge, reason, explain, plan, for machine learning, and with natural language. This is where AIEd was. This is what thrived. AI educational assets did not depend on excellent modeling. Their use depended on the organization's context for use. As acceptance and deployment of AIEd continues, education will broaden the horizons. It will use AI to support higher level learning. AI is dynamic by nature. This distinguishes it from other technologies.

Intelligent Tutor Systems (ITS) are valuable for learning well-defined knowledge and skills. New ITS will move away from closed domains and tutoring tasks. Higher order learning requires arguing, describing and explaining. It requires predicting, analyzing, assessing and synthesizing. Traditional ITS provides support of knowing and doing. The learning environment plays an important part in connecting higher levels of learning and AI. Learning science and research supports the fact that learning does not take place in isolation. Social activities are critical for developing thinking. Interactions are a critical part of any learning environment (Andriessen & Sandberg, 1999).

The ideas on knowledge are shifting. What AI can support and how it gets supported are intertwined with pedagogy, linguistics and social contexts. The inclusion of "Big Data" and the restructuring of data from file cabinets to data lakes has opened up possibilities for AIEd. Access to the data is much more flexible. Using the data is easier. Data for AI and learning is not static. It is everchanging and growing. The evolution of AI requires ongoing research in both the Education and AI fields. The view of what knowledge is stands intricately woven into the perceptions of how to teach. Facts and opinions are distinctly different. Knowledge is either universally objective and factual or local, subjective and personal. That knowledge is transmitted by telling characterizes most educational systems. It is top down, authoritarian and judgmental. The wisdom of the expert is used as the "bar" against which the learner is measured. It is rather outdated with AI in the house. There is no question that huge gaps exist between AI, the educational community and learning sciences and that even bigger opportunities exist.

Individual and Real

Personalized learning has become more available because of technologies. Until recently, independent learning was not linked to technologies. Research, done in the early 1960s, supports that we relate to screens on a one-to-one basis. Learning models like "apprentice and mentor" stress one-to-one relationships. Many technologies in the last few decades target learning outcomes. Learning can be customized with preferences and progress. Monitoring learner behavior can help the instructor as well as the learner. Each can progress at a pace that is comfortable and effective. Individualized learning adds flexibility. It adapts to each learner. It tries to recognize different learning styles, cognitive skills, preferences and differences.

In traditional classrooms learners are grouped by level. The instructor changes content and approach based on skills and preferences. Moving forward system designers will do this. They will make learning environments immersive and real. There will be more connection between platforms. More functions will be tailored to specific content. Intelligent adaption can and will help to facilitate the learning process. Innovative learning is flexible. Learner centered environments are based on monitoring progress, preference and using learning science (Al-Hudhud, 2012).

Chatbots and Personal Assistants

Chatbots and Personal Assistants are software applications that are developed to mimic human conversation. Their purpose is to connect with a real person. Chatbots are springing up everywhere. From healthcare to human resources, a bot is there to help. The intent of these technologies is to simplify the conversation between computer and human. Their first area of impact was in customer service.

They have the ability to both track conversations and impart information. These technologies play an increasing role in customer service and as support.

The Internet brought expectations of 24/7 answers. These new expectations include immediate, personalized, and accessible responses. We expect a response regardless of the time of day. Based on rules, bots have become economically accessible and easy to build. These technologies simulate human language. They are built to use informal styles and have their own personality. They can also understand written and spoken language. And they can interpret its meaning. In AIEd, these technologies usually show up as tutors. They assist learners with various tasks and create interactions (Sienkiewicz, 2020).

Adaptive Learning Adaptive Learning (AL) has the potential to be of great value. It customizes learning environments to the individual. It integrates prior knowledge and accounts for individual progress. Sherry Turkle from MIT is the author of several books including *Alone Together*. Sherry believes that technology-based learning environments are limited. Learners can only thrive face-to-face. However, as technology improves, learning science is challenging this. AI has the potential to personalize, individualize and adapt. Most of what has happened so far has been trial and error. There is a need for sound research and proven techniques of instruction. 75% of learners report that using AL is helpful. They like it for learning new concepts and making them aware of previously unknown concepts.

Adaptive environments are included in some LMS (Learning Management System) technologies. In AL classes, adaptive and required assignments are combined. Research suggests that instructor interactions are desirable. AL can be used to collect data. This provides insight and leads to more engaging interactions and instructor outreach. AL can provide insight into learner habits and open new opportunities for learning. There are many chances to create new instructional approaches, based on feedback and data (Sloan and Anderson, 2018).

Virtual Reality

Virtual Reality (VR) will also bring new learning environments. One model appropriate for this kind of technology is the studio model. In this model the student is responsible for the learning not the teacher. Learners are encouraged to experiment, create, make mistakes and do it again. The more constructive and varied the efforts, the more learning that takes place. More than learning facts and skills, learners are learning how to learn. They apply what they learn and put it into practice. They have the flexibility to apply it to new scenarios and situations. Learners can plan, monitor and adjust the ongoing learning process. Virtual reality has so far had limited applications in education. There are many reasons including culture and costs. The main issue lies in the education itself. In a studio or lab environment the role of the expert and the learner are switched. Learners initiate new learning experiences. Experts are expected to coach not lecture or teach (Andriessen & Sandberg, 1999).

Virtual Reality provides authentic immersive experiences. It can simulate the real world which may not be accessible to the learner. The environment might be dangerous. It may be expensive or limited by time or geography. Often what if scenarios are played out in VR. This is so the learner can transfer the knowledge to real world situations.

VR becomes intelligent when it is enhanced with AI. With AI it can interact with and respond to actions, voice and even intent. It can provide support and guidance on the journey through VR. This helps the learner to align with the learning objectives. Learners can be confused or overwhelmed. VR agents may also provide alternative views, feedback, questions and perspectives. Emerging AI in VR has been researched. It is proven to provide enhanced educational outcomes. It supports learners being able to construct their own understanding and explore (Luckin, et al., 2016)

Augmented Reality

Augmented Reality (AR) Systems go one step beyond VR. AR allows learners and instructors to interact differently with the world around them. AR can support physical and emotional well-being. It can also support cognitive development (Luckin, et al., 2016). AR combines computer-generated information with the learner's view of the real world. It provides an aggregated view. It works with vision-based recognition algorithms. It is based on sensory input. It enhances reality with sound, video, graphics and other inputs using a computer or a mobile device.

Universal Design

In Universal Design (UD) learners receive different kinds of support for their own learning. They can choose the pathways and strategies customized to their needs. AI has the potential to be very important in UD. AI can support learning environments that offer many different didactic approaches. AI can offer multiple versions of the material. It can offer multiple explanations, adaptive interpretation and a variety of learner support tools. AI has the potential to address all three neural networks usually associated with UD. This includes recognition of "what" learners learn, prior knowledge and their feelings. UD also impacts the motivation to learn (Andriessen & Sandberg, 1999).

AI and Jobs in Education

AI is beginning to change education. It is affecting instructional approaches, tools and institutions. It is changing the future. This will impact best practices and the role of the instructor and jobs (Marr, 2018). AI has already been applied to developing workplace skills and testing. It will continue to evolve and drive efficiency and individualization, and take over redundant administrative tasks. AI will not replace instructors in the near future. It will support interactions between learners and teachers based on data and learning science. The vision for learning is one where instructors and AI work together to improve learning outcomes. It is important for the education sector to adapt AI. Current generations will encounter it in the workplace now and even more so in the future. AIEd has the potential to meet an individual's needs. More digital tools and platforms are being developed daily. AI can identify knowledge gaps and provide feedback and remediation. AI can help to break down silos between traditional educational channels and the workplace.

The penetration of AI into the workforce, on whatever the scale, implies the necessity for continuous learning. The new "Agile Workplace" will require unprecedented access to training materials and instruction on new roles and jobs. Workers will need to update their skills regularly. They will need to move into and out of new professions and positions. As more and more jobs become automated, workers will need to retrain for positions (Baggio & Omana, 2019).

AI will impact a variety of segments of many economies differently. It will affect some quickly and some more slowly. Very few will remain untouched. As this unfolds, the trick will be to stay ahead of AI's ability to act autonomously. Learning can also help workers keep a sense of purpose and personal accomplishment in their lives (Lee, 2018). Workers will be forced to change occupations, some every few years. Currently, we are uncertain about the pace and path of automation, but many will be replaced in jobs they've held for a lifetime.

Education appears to be the best solution to AI related employment problems. The scale and speed of AI adaption will not provide the luxury of passive education improvement. Other scenarios like work sharing and income support have been put on the table by people like Larry Page, co-founder of Google. Undoubtably AI will have short-term and long-term effects on the labor market. AI holds the threat of long term, persistent, nonstop diffusion of jobs. Income redistribution is on the table and may solve some of the pain. Longer-term solutions for radical measures might be needed. Governments will need creativity and open minds to generate innovative solutions.

Education needs to plan. No one knows exactly how this will play out. Cognitive technologies will perform many tasks with a great deal of autonomy. It is likely that AI will create significant upheaval in job markets. New skills will be required. New jobs will be created. New opportunities will exist. What can be done is learning from the past. We can examine current jobs to evaluate the likelihood of AI automation in the near future (Davenport, 2019).

The mass of data collected in AIEd systems can help to provide evidence for viable approaches. Just in Time (JIT) and PoW (Point of Work) feedback will interact with learner challenges, successes and needs. Assessment and evaluation will take place while learning is taking place, instead of after the fact. New discoveries in psychology and neuroscience will support a better understanding of learning. AIEd needs to create comfortable and motivated lifelong learners. Educational models and systems need to change. Most significantly, there will be more questions than answers as AIEd moves forward.

The sharing of data is imperative to AIEd moving forward. AIEd has the potential to reach students and help close the achievement gap. The gap exists between learners from more affluent and poorer backgrounds. It has the potential to measure educational system achievement in ways that are unique. AI will be able to provide feedback and analysis on every level of teaching and learning. It won't matter whether it is a class, a lesson, a subject, a university, state or country. Educational systems will need to be agile and committed to reform. It's all about the learning, not about AI technology alone. The evolution needs to be funded, supported, innovative and collaborative. Standards will play an important role in AIEd. More teachers, professors, trainers and learners need to be involved in the development of AIEd tools. They especially need to be involved in developing the rules that will govern ethics and data sharing.

ASK THE HARD QUESTIONS

- How is AI being used in training and education today?
- How might AI help underprivileged learners?
- How to we guard privacy and personal information in AIEd?
- Can our current educational systems adapt to AI?
- How do you feel about AI for education and training?

Chapter 9

Blockchain Edu

"Code alone is just a tool. It is humans that must lead."
—Alex Tapscott

Blockchain is a narrow version of DTL, Distributed Ledger Technology. A blockchain is a chronological record of transactions, recorded and cryptographically linked to the previous record, forming a chain. Three key characteristics of blockchain are integrity, transparency and democracy. This was first created to serve the financial industry. Distributed Ledger Technologies and blockchain are now disrupting industry after industry and igniting innovation. These technologies have sparked praise, criticism, wonder, investment and fast-moving revolutions. The education community is scurrying to leverage blockchain technologies. They can address the issues of data sharing and transparency in schools, companies and institutions. Blockchain combined with AI is very powerful.

Integrity refers to the fact that records in the blockchain are cryptographically linked and are nearly impossible to alter. This helps to ensure the integrity of the data and opens up opportunities for new ways of storing and sharing digital credentials. Identity protocols combined with other technologies can provide transparency, utility and trust. These unique identity conventions benefit risk management and impact privacy. Blockchain is an exciting new technology that coupled with AI is just beginning to be explored.

Blockchain has the potential to add validity and security to student data for assessment and credentialing. It is an append-only architecture. It is impossible to reverse a transaction on a blockchain.

Transparency is foundational to blockchain. It is based on the knowledge of two facts: who owns the asset and who participated in forming the contract. It has this ability because of a distributed infrastructure. Blockchain might provide a connection between formal learning, non-formal learning and informal learning processes. Blockchain databases are secure, distributed and accessible. They provide the learner with more autonomy in monitoring their own learning strategies. They can help learners optimize their time. They may have the ability to create their own ecosystem of interactions and relationships. The 21st century has different needs for learning and must support new pathways. Blockchain has the flexibility to provide the learner with opportunities to create their own environment of interactions and relationships. It can support lifelong constructivist and collectivist environments.

Democracy is also an important characteristic of blockchain. There is no one centralized authority. Data is not stored in one location. It is distributed to allow peer to peer transactions without a centralized mediator. Blockchain is a trust protocol that eliminates the need for firewalls. It links all transactions and gives them a permanent time stamp. There is no way to reverse a transaction. It works with a series of keys, private or public, and the information transmitted. There is no single authority, central owner, back door dealings or central server involved. Blockchain is very clever code, mass collaboration and cryptology.

The potential for learning environments is huge. So far, education and L&D are moving slowly towards the adoption of these technologies. Part of it is the spend, part of it is understanding and part of it is cultures resistant to change. There are huge benefits on the horizon if blockchain can be adopted to support innovation and transform learning networks (PTAC, 2019).

Whose Credentials Are They?

Education is slow to adapt to change especially in the areas of new technologies. There is no doubt that blockchain can help education move forward by application in digital credentialing. This is a first step and a good place to start using blockchain. Blockchain could be used to store digital credentials like certificates, badges and qualifications. The potential is there to track actual learning accomplishments at the learning level for the individual. Blockchain can make them accessible without the intervention and fees associated with centralized ledger systems.

Blockchain would support decreasing the role of the intermediary and decentralizing control to the learners. The process of certification and managing false records can be handled using blockchain with end-to-end encryption. The authentication processes can be developed to assure privacy and maintain integrity and transparency.

Traditional learning environments are not the only ones that will benefit highly from blockchain. Open and distance learning will need to adapt this fairly quickly because the benefits to business will be significant. Blockchain offers the ability to combine educational resources and provide a competitive advantage. It can aid in effective decision making and bridge the gaps between priorities, models and effective practice. Blockchain has the ability to help predict future trends and reach market demands.

Pathways to Employment

Education and training can benefit tremendously from the characteristic of blockchain known as sharing. It can be used to allow education to reach people beyond institutions and organizations and in countries that currently lack access. It can certainly ease the process of validating credentials and certificates and help ensure transparency and quality in education. Performance and reliability go hand in hand with transparency and confidentiality. It's not that the application of blockchain to education will be without issues. But the benefits to long term improvement can outweigh the challenges. Areas like individual privacy, profiling, reframing skills, performance, inclusion, distribution and regulation will have to be explored thoroughly.

Blockchains have a natural place in tracking, managing and authenticating activities in online platforms especially in MOOCs (Massive Online Open Courses). MOOCs have a notoriously small completion rate and blockchain might be used as a motivational tool. Most importantly, blockchain has the potential to increase trust in learning. There are still many challenges to overcome but the benefits can be huge for enriching the experience of learners on all levels (Pulist, 2021).

Clear learning pathways can be another benefit from blockchain. Blockchains can be developed on a community level to match schools and employers to provide an education to employment pipelines. If everyone joins in and uses the same blockchain, the possibilities are exponential. The ability to transfer credits easily between community colleges and four-year institutions can be immediate.

The same is true with employment. Employers can see detailed information including degrees and academic records such as courses taken, topics covered and outcomes. This allows an employer to evaluate learning with a more contextual view. Blockchain has many possibilities if people can come together and commit to a shared program and common framework. It creates trust and requires standardization. It can reduce the administrative burden for HR and academic institutions.

It can also help Higher Education in the dissemination and authentication of research and intellectual property. It can provide a platform between institutions, researchers and public and private organizations. This can help with ensuring academic integrity and identifying where ideas really begin.

The biggest benefits for adopting blockchain are for the learners. Learners can have the ability to have learning recognized wherever it occurs... in a classroom, on the job, self-directed or in service to others. Blockchain has the potential to create a unified ecosystem(s), bringing together learning done in one's free time with more formal learning environments.

One of the big challenges for blockchain finding its way into the world of education is the upfront costs. The cost of Internet access became apparent with the 2019 COVID outbreak. There are large social and economic disparities of access to the Internet.

Privacy and SSI Identification

Blockchain is built on the principles of self-sovereign identity (SSI). It can help learners manage their records by increasing control, access and transparency. Not all SSI systems are blockchain.

SSI is a set of principles that support individual control over identifying information including online credentials. A person generally has multiple sets of identifying credentials from a variety of systems and applications they interact with online. How many and how different these identifiers are can be confusing, frustrating and difficult to manage. Instead of a password and a user ID, SSI promotes a digital identity based on principles that create trust and assurance. The ten principles of SSI are an independent existence, user control of identity, access to your own data, systems and algorithms are transparent, identities are persistent and long lived, information and services about identity are transportable, they are as widely used as possible, users give consent for use of their identity, minimize disclosure and user rights are protected.

Blockchain is a technology that enables SSI.

FERPA (Federal Educational Rights and Privacy Act) and SSI share common principles. They embrace empowering people to be informed of the information collected on them. They provide access to its use for specific purposes and assure that the data is correct and protected. Consent to share data under FERPA requires a consent form detailing a specific purpose. Individuals have the right to challenge false or misleading information and request it be amended. FERPA has put consent and security standards into play for sharing data. There is an opt in or opt out requirement for sharing data that supports transparency and openness. While FERPA recognizes the central authority as owning the records, it states that individuals must have access to those records. SSI goes even further and might provide a host of controls to enable the user to decide exactly what data is shared. Data minimization is another aspect shared between FERPA and SSI, and states that only required elements of data be collected and retained. Another aspect of each is transparency about the use and purpose of sharing data (Allen, 2016).

Currently, blockchain is not widely used in education. When it is, it is used for storing and sharing academic records. Blockchain will begin to make a mark on education for more than credentialling. Blockchain has the ability to change the focus of education and put the learner in the center. In 2019 Credential Engine conducted research that stated more than 738,000 unique credentials are used to document learning. These are degrees, certificates, badges, apprenticeships, PEUs, CEUs and a variety of other records. Lifelong learning will become more and more vital as we move toward the Agile workplace.

Blockchain by its very nature is resistant to fraud. Records in a blockchain can't be altered only amended by adding a new block. This makes changing or falsifying an ongoing academic record difficult to do. Learners and educators can store syllabi and coursework securely. Blockchain is perfect for levels of mastery by assigning smart contracts. In the smart contract the instructor lays out the sequence and once an assignment is completed satisfactorily the next assignment is automatically provided for the learner.

The same kind of smart contract can be used in grading and make the entire process more learner centered and less subjective. Education can also use blockchain to share content with folks outside of the institution (like parents, employers and accreditors) so that education is no longer a black box. Feedback can be shared both ways in the blockchain... from the instructor to the learner and from the learner back to the institution. Most importantly it can open up new and more affordable pathways by disrupting the relationships between schools, learners and employers.

At the university level, financial departments are labor intensive and complicated. They involve students, parents, scholarship funds, federal and state loans, private loans and a massive amount of overhead and bureaucracy. Blockchain and AI automation can solve this problem and maybe even lower tuition. The more career sites that support blockchain credentials and links to employment the sooner the shift will come for education. Zip Recruiter and Upwork are only two examples of sites already supporting its adoption.

Although there are challenges and plenty of them, the U.S. Department of Education's Education Blockchain Initiative Action Network and the American Council on Education's Education Blockchain Initiative (EBI) bring together invested parties to collaborate on how this can change the future of education. EBI is starting with record sharing. This will speed up the connection between institutions and employers. The approach gives ownership of the credentials to learners not the institutions. Blockchain supports learner control over their own digital identities and lifelong learning process. The next step will be to simplify college entry and credit transfers (Maryville, 2020).

Lifelong Learning and Blockchain

Education has transformed into a lifelong pursuit. Individuals are training and retraining as technologies and the market for skills requires in order to further their careers. The number of years an individual stays in the workforce is also increasing. Regular and continuous professional development is a key to remaining productive and to long-term employment. Options to support the demand for lifelong learning are growing rapidly.

Online learning, credentialing, and work-based training are providing opportunities for continuous professional growth. Currently, data about an individual is stored in many different systems. Each set of systems has different rules on privacy and access. Limiting the data that is stored in and across these systems can help reduce security risks for the individual and the institutions. Blockchain can help solve this. Blockchain technology is essentially a ledger of data stored across computers linked together using cryptographic technology in a way that makes it impossible to tamper with the data on a chain. Instead of storing sensitive data on the chain, it could act as an index and the credentials could reside off chain with a directory of keys or indexes that point to them. In this way blockchain can reduce the need for centralized control of student data. It can reduce the need to store individual data in third party private systems not regulated by federal law, which is one way that personal data becomes vulnerable to poor security practices (PTAC, 2021).

Much of the data remain siloed behind the walls of institutions and HR departments. This causes a time and financial burden on the learner. The more learning opportunities they indulge in the harder it is to collect the credentials from each individual institution or organization. Blockchain offers a solution that is both verifiable and protects an individual's journey through education and the workforce. Digitizing the entire verification process will save money and time for individuals seeking verification and for institutions trying to meet that demand.

Education is More Than Just School

Almost 50% of all jobs are at risk of AI transformation in the next few years. Big changes in the labor market are putting more pressure on traditional and new education providers. There are many moving parts: K-12, Higher Education, public workforce programs, employers, non-profits, for profits etc. The number of credentials being offered has skyrocketed. In the U.S. alone there are 7,133 credentials from MOOC providers, 370,000 from post-secondary institutions and 315,067 from nonacademic organizations (Lemoie and Soares, 2020). There is exponential growth across all providers but especially new and short-term education/training programs. Blockchain is a perfect solution for sharable human capital portfolios. Verifiable transcripts and CVs can match employers and applicants and include life experiences for the complex needs of both. Workday Credentials is an example of a verifiable blockchain based platform.

Blockchain offers connected educational ecosystems the benefit of trust. ODEM is a European network developed to match skills, competencies, qualifications and jobs to connect job seekers with job openings. Schools in Texas, Arizona and other states are creating education ecosystems because they offer connection. Dallas Community College District stands out in this effort and is an example of how blockchain can help us address social equity issues. Blockcerts is one of the first frameworks to offer a verifiable type of credential to blockchain. Developed in 2016 by MIT and Hyland Labs, it uses a QR code to verify credentials without reliance on the issuing institution. Verifiable credentials (VCs) are also being used in public libraries.

The power of distributed ledger technologies for education lies in building trust. Trust framework policy can determine how data is managed, stored and verified. Common Education Data Standards (CEDS) facilitates sharing data between programs, institutions, districts and states. Supported by NCES (National Center for Education Statistics) the vocabulary and data model describe organizations, accreditations, credentials and competencies. It sets an example for how to build trust with distributed leger technologies. DCC (Digital Credentials Consortium) is a multi-university project focused on storing, displaying and verifying digital credentials. And this is only the beginning.

Implementation of digital ledger technologies in education is at the startup stage. Although it is springing up here and there, it is not yet being widely used. Hiring managers and registrars don't trust digital credentials and are not sure how to evaluate them. The perceived benefits have not yet outweighed the costs. Data ownership can be muddy. There are laws like FERPA (Family Education Rights and Privacy Act) and GDPR (General Data Protection Act) that make ownership cloudy. In centralized systems this is much clearer. The information is owned by the owner of the server hosting the data. In decentralized systems the data is controlled by whoever owns the private key associated with the transaction, but this doesn't necessarily equate to ownership. Learners with a verifiable key have control over the data but they don't own it unless they issued the credential. If they lose the key, they lose control of the data.

Connecting existing relationships builds the foundation for trust. Building ecosystems first can lay a foundation for mutually beneficial support. Mutually beneficial support can produce evidence and scaffold the development of decentralized frameworks, systems and software. Building on existing trust is the key to adoption and acceptance. Eventually, the technology will improve and be easier to use. Eventually, the concepts will become more familiar to stakeholders and the benefits more apparent. Blockchain is all about building connection to assure trust by machines working together. Blockchain can initiate new ways of thinking about ownership, use and control of data.

Education isn't just about learning. It is also about documenting, verifying and sharing evidence that learning has occurred. Distributed ledger technologies are sustainable, transparent and auditable while maintaining security and privacy, making them perfect for consensus and transaction driven data. Data ownership and privacy are imperative to vulnerable populations. We still live in a world where not everyone has access to the Internet or technology. According to Pew Research, 29% of Americans do not have smartphones, 49% don't have broadband and 46% don't own a computer (Lemoie and Soares, 2020).

Lifelong learning is a new guiding principle because we have a workplace that is changing quickly and dramatically. Stakeholder ecosystems bring organizations together and move information across institutional boundaries. Research shows that these ecosystems are foundational to early adoption experiments in blockchain because they bring in preestablished trust. Distributed ledger technology can define a new relationship between individuals, institutions and employers and the data, documents and credentials that follow individuals throughout their lives (Lemoie and Soares, 2020).

Gatekeeper Confidence

Since the University of Bologna was established in Italy in 1088 A.D. society has put its faith in Higher Education as a trusted institution to issue credentials. For a long time, it was unchallenged. People had faith in these institutions as gatekeepers of knowledge. They trusted their integrity and valued their credentials. In 1995 something changed. When the Internet came onto the scene in 1995, it opened doors to learning. Online Higher Education took time and space out of the equation. Student loan debt continued to increase. Where people went for information changed. You could Google it. You could find everything online. Tuition continued to soar. New models of education began to spring up. Our faith in Higher Education as the gatekeeper for creating new knowledge, distributing existing knowledge and preserving prior knowledge changed (Baggio, 2017).

As long as employers, governments and society at large continue to value Higher Education credentials we will be willing to pay for them. Higher Education will remain the gatekeepers for opportunity. But outdated pedagogy and an unwillingness to change to new ways of learning has put a dent in credibility even at the most prestigious schools. "A lecture has become the process in which the notes of the teacher go to the notes of the student without going through the brains of either" (Tapscott and Tapscott, 2017, p. 26).

Standards of trust and accreditation like academic tenure and the Carnegie hour are being challenged. New models of learning continue to spring up. Models that are professional, transferable, stackable, experiential, chunk-able and credentialed. It's not just about knowledge or transferable skills anymore, it's about the ability to continue to learn throughout a lifetime. The changes we face and continue to face with AI moving at lightning speed require an ability to problem solve, collaborate and communicate. Roles are being redefined not in terms of job descriptions but in terms of dynamic tenets. Organizations are becoming more agile. Everyone owns a piece of everything and is responsible for success. The watch words are agile, open and consensus.

Blockchain and AI together are incredibly powerful. They offer employers the ability to match projects with proven capabilities. They can match Human Resource training with increased capabilities and return on investments. Higher Education hasn't changed. It is relatively isolated and disconnected. It offers scholarship. It has not yet used advancing technologies effectively to break down the division between institutions, professors, industry, parents and students. This will require institutions to make deep structural changes quickly. Time is not on their side. Blockchain offers trust, security and integrity and the ability to create a global network of learning accreditation without walls. Currently, most institutions see very little reason to change even though change is pounding on their door. The widespread adoption of the Internet caused them to lose their monopoly on knowledge. They still own educational brands and credentialing. But how long can this last? How long until the gatekeepers lose trust and the old immovable paradigm crumbles? Blockchain and AI together offer a promising future for learning and global networking that threatens to replace an old, outdated and expensive system for learning.

ASK THE HARD QUESTIONS

- How long will it be before we see blockchain in education?
- How do you think it will show up? Do you think there will be resistance?
- How do you think Lifelong Learning will impact blockchain adoption?
- Does blockchain have a place in K-12?
- What are the benefits of a learning to employment pathway?

Chapter 10

Robotic Process Automation

"Just because you can, doesn't mean you should."
—Anonymous

Robotic Process Automation (RPA) is a form of software automation. It is used to mimic and replace redundant back-office tasks such as data entry, confirmation and moving information around. It uses scripts that imitate human processes. RPA completes various activities using autonomous tools. It moves transactions across a number of unrelated software systems. In theory it provides the "glue" between enterprise and productivity applications. RPA is based on rules. It handles high volume repetitive work. RPA frees up humans for more complex tasks. The reasons for using RPA are simple. RPA accelerates the digital change, increases ROI and decreases staff expenses.

IA (Intelligent Automation) is the reverse version of AI. IA is RPA with some AI tossed in, or strategically placed to enhance operations. IA can also be referred to as IPA (Intelligent Process Automation). Confused? You're not alone. Machine learning, natural language processing and computer vision are examples of incorporating subdisciplines to enhance RPA. This pushes RPA beyond simple rules. IA is about doing, thinking and learning. Using algorithms and data, software automation can make decisions and perform faster and more efficiently.

AI and IA are not the same thing. Oftentimes they are mistaken for each other, intentionally or not so intentionally. RPA is process driven and AI is data driven. RPA bots follow the processes designed by humans. It's what they do. AI bots use patterns in data to learn over time. RPA replicates tasks while AI is intended to simulate human intelligence. The way in which they automate processes is also different (Casey, 2021).

RPA is Different

RPA differs from other forms of automation. It supports data handled in and between multiple applications. In traditional workflow automations, the software engineer makes a list of the tasks to automate. The next step is to connect the systems using APIs (Application Program Interfaces). These are usually produced internally. In contrast, RPA develops the action list by watching the user perform that task. RPA then repeats those tasks where the user performs them. RPA handles data in and between several applications. An example is receiving a customer service request in chat. RPA extracts the data, and then types that data into a customer service application.

RPA software has many possibilities. It can decrease the coding to build automated scripts. It can integrate the enterprise. It can combine data design, monitoring and security. It can reach through legacy systems. It can combine data through front end applications. It can replace human workers by performing routine tasks like logging into multiple systems, and copying and pasting from one system to another. RPA is valuable because it can quickly integrate. It presents one solution on the front end as well as connecting data and enterprise web services.

There are many potential benefits to RPA: less coding, rapid cost savings, higher consumer satisfaction, better accuracy and compliance. RPA can work while old systems stay in place. RPA doesn't disrupt underlying systems. RPA bots work on the presentation layer, or GUI (Graphic User Interface). Business can implement bots where no API exists and without doing deep system integration (Lawton, 2021).

RPA has many challenges. One of the most significant is organizational culture. Organizations can eliminate jobs and displace workers. Organizations need to promote learning and change because RPA shifts job roles and responsibilities. Processes in companies are hard to change. People like to stick with the familiar and the known. Automation and digital transformation require workers to adapt to new and shifting priorities. Another challenge is scale. Bots are easier to implement on a small and isolated level.

Few RPA initiatives progress beyond 10 bots. More than 30% of all bots currently in use are used in the financial industry. Banks can deploy thousands of bots to manage transactions. Banks use RPA up and down the line to manage high-volume data entry. Financial processes entail a surplus of rule based and redundant tasks. RPA automation simplifies this. Insurance is another area that is full of repetitive processes and perfect for RPA. Claims processing, regulatory compliance, policy management, and underwriting are all tasks suited for RPA. Health care is another transaction-oriented segment. It uses RPAs to manage information like insurance claims, prescription management, payment cycles and other processes. Retail has been shaken to the core by ecommerce. Bots have been a big part of it. Bots will continue to play very important roles in retail. RPA is used for supply chain management, warehousing, order fulfillment and processing customer feedback (IBM, 2021).

RPA stands for Robotic Process Automation. What it actually does many times is automate tasks, not processes. More effort and complexity might be required to knit those tasks into processes. RPA is often controlled by the "Rule of Five." The Rule of Five states that RPA tends to break down when a bot has to make more than 5 decisions, or if bot interfaces with more than 5 applications or manipulates more than 500 clicks.

Although they can help with security, RPA can also be the gateway to security problems. If a bot is compromised, it can pose an increased security risk. Bots are not resilient. They don't change when the outside world causes changes in business processes. Bots require a variety of QA/QC (Quality Assurance and Quality Control) processes to ensure they work as intended. This is typically limited by human input. There can also be challenges to privacy requirements. This is true for personally identifiable information.

RPA is about bots mimicking the behavior of and replacing humans. RPA can provide cost savings, speed, accuracy, consistency, quality and even increased security. RPA offers a solution to difficult, costly and complex problems. Legacy systems can have variable and customized rules. RPA replaces humans on the back end for data entry and processing. Many of these solutions are possible because of virtual technology. This eliminates the need for more hardware and lowers costs. RPA is changing the cost structure for the service industries. The prices of products and services continue to decrease. The levels of quality service, outcomes and personalization continue to increase.

RPA disrupts outsourcing. Business Process Outsourcing (BPO) is changing. What does the future hold? No one knows. There are many variables. Some BPO issues are onshore, offshore and who owns the intellectual property of RPA. Hyper automation is even more complex. Hyper automation combines RPA with AI, ML and Process Mining to impact outcomes. An example is voice recognition software combined with digital dictation to allow for processing without manual intervention. Other examples are chatbots used to service online retailers' customer service requests, and voice responsive chatbots integrated with travel scheduling software that suggest the cheapest flights. Hyper automation allows the technology to capture more context from the content (Dilmegani, 2020).

RPA is growing in popularity. Why? Because it can reduce costs. Business doesn't have to change the underlying IT structure to bring in RPA. People don't have to learn new tools. RPA doesn't need to ask IT for support. RPA can break, however, when the underlying processes and/or application interfaces change. Scaling RPA across an enterprise usually requires integration. It requires centralized IT governance and management. RPA requires less expertise to use than API or low-code development. Simple bots record clicks and capture keystrokes. More sophisticated bots can read the back end of screens and create their own process and workflow. Some have integrated process mining applications that automatically map common enterprise flows. More sophisticated bots have AI incorporated. RPA can ensure that business operations and processes comply with regulations and standards. Bots digitize and standardize auditing processes and ultimately help workers to be more productive (IBM, 2021).

RPA and Hyper Automation

The future of RPA is blossoming. There is no question that RPA can be useful to organizations with different and sophisticated systems. RPA's growth will be accelerated by hyper automation. Process and task mining will help to identify new ways to use RPA. AI will make it easier to use those automations. AI governance tools will help enterprises monitor RPA. Governance tools will manage the overall process of streamlining processes. The collective impact will save companies billions in the near future (Lawton, 2021).

RPA that is scalable can be managed from a central control point rather than set up and scaled on each device. RPA can go fast, and the business can test, design and optimize new processes in a few hours. RPA is reliable if bots have built in monitoring and display the health of the system. Simple is also important to RPA success. The RPA product should be simple enough for employees in the business to build and use. Simple RPA can handle turning data into information and enable good decisions. Finally, the product should have intelligent capabilities. It should be scalable, reliable and manageable. Security credentials, privacy issues and compliance are essential capabilities. These depend on the industry. Ideally the bot should be able to justify itself by logging the usage. This gives you the ability to calculate ROI and estimated value.

Leadership will be responsible for determining if these tools are helping reach the business's goals. The C-level executives who own the processes that RPA will automate need to all work together. This will assure an enterprise secure platform for operating RPA across systems.

RPA is Evolving

RPA is artificial intelligence or voice/text recognition software. It can open emails and attachments, log in to enterprise systems, move files and folders and copy and paste. RPA can read and write to databases, scrape for data, connect to API (Application Program Interface) and make calculations. It can extract data from documents and follow decision tree rules. Oh, and it can connect to social media statistics. It is making physical white collar knowledge work obsolete, except maybe for sales. RPA can interact with user interfaces just like humans do. It has opened a very wide range of options for the workplace.

What really makes RPA a superpower now and different from basic business process automation is it is flexible, easily integrated and implemented and cost-effective. RPA is much less expensive than humans doing the same tasks. BPO solutions are no longer economical and make no sense. Many of firms saw the writing on the wall and embraced RPA. Now they have become RPA outsourcing firms and can be very effective because of economies of scale. Some RPA relies on humans to watch it and some does not. Hybrid RPA is a combination of both attended and unattended. What does all of this mean for the workplace? Big, huge, gigantic changes.

When it is implemented well, RPA can free up workers from mindless tasks and give them time for more productive activities. The term "robotic" doesn't mean a physical machine, it means software. RPA is great for predefined, redundant, structured low level rote tasks. It can conquer electronic filing forms, process transactions, and send messages. It can easily eliminate drudgery in HR onboarding, billing management, order processing and data entry. Banks use it for processing loans, invoices, and checks. Sales uses it for invoicing and quotes, and insurance uses it to process claims. But that's not all.

RPA also has evolved to include process mining, bot creation tools, plug ins for connecting to enterprise systems, scheduling and orchestration.

RPA fails because vendors overpromise and underperform. Companies don't really understand or define the processes they want to automate before they select the RPA tools. RPA works by pulling information out of existing systems either from the front end or the back end. In many legacy systems it's the front end because the back is not accessible. Front end RPA is evolved "screen scraping" and relies on machine learning to reduce although not eliminate showstoppers like updated screens or numbers that are too large. Once it gets what it needs it goes on to do the next "predetermined" task like sending an invoice, email or report. It really can increase business capacity when the rate-limiting tasks are automated.

Humans are In Charge

Ultimately, it still falls to humans to define the workflow up front. Humans are also in charge of process recording and writing and editing scripts. Sometimes IT sets up the flow and sometimes flow-chart-like choices are available so that "digital citizens" can develop the process flow. The most difficult aspect of reproducing business processes for automation is defining what the business processes are to begin with and why they exist. Sometimes process mining tools can help with this and sometimes it has to be done manually.

Choosing an RPA product and vendor is not easy. All vendors have priority file structures and there are no standards for RPA. Careful evaluation up front and doing a proof of concept can save pain and money. Before committing to anything do the homework because changing your mind can be a disaster and be very expensive. Look at the features and look at the work environment without rose-colored glasses. Build sample scripts and create a proof of concept for as many possible scenarios as is realistic. Don't just tackle the easy stuff. Use the tools that are provided and make sure the orchestration works. Go through the entire process flow in detail and then do it again and again. There needs to be a wide range of different personas tested and a low code environment for developing bots and business rules. Finally, it might be helpful to have professional programmers look at how they might write real automation code to call the RPA tools APIs. Then ask the hard questions like how it handled exceptions and how much human review was really involved.

Generally, these bots will work off of limits and probability rules (Heller, 2021). Somewhere between those boundaries is room for human judgment, and it is important that the RPA tool recognizes this and is capable of submitting the case for human review. It's very important to do the work up front. If an organization selects the wrong vendor, it can be disastrous. If the RPA system isn't implemented right and needs capabilities it doesn't have or are missing, it's not easy to switch. Testing and process evaluation up front and in depth are essential. Documenting each step of the RPA process including creating each bot might help. Remember, with RPA, not AI, humans are in charge of defining the flow.

New vendors for RPA are springing up all the time. The challenges for organizations are usually internal. RPA will facilitate the automation of flow between existing infrastructure and systems, but humans have to figure out what that is. The main reason for implementing RPA is to maximize profit and minimize workload. Implementing RPA can become a large-scale, long-term nightmare if the processes and testing are not done well (Rajan, 2021).

Another challenge to RPA's success is the systems it tries to link together automatically. It is critical the business has systems that can uphold the RPA tools so that accurate output can be generated from them. Timely updates and monitoring are necessary because the technologies move quickly, and RPA should be able to withstand changes. RPA failures can come in many forms like bot failure, system error or unexpected random issues. It's important to have someone monitoring the RPA and keeping an eye out for systemic failures.

Finally, another issue is using RPA where RPA really isn't the answer. It is very important to review and audit RPA. Sometimes RPA is assigned to a non-repetitive task leading to unnecessary costs. The most formative challenge to successfully implementing RPA is identifying the kinds of tasks it will do. Next is identifying the tasks and the process flow for each option. There are research-based indexes that calculate a score for RPA suitability. They provide guidelines to organizations making the transition to RPA. Processes with high workload and low complexity are good candidates for RPA. The business function and the industry are also important. If a business process is easy to define, standard and repetitive, and follows well-defined rules, RPA might be a good fit. If it is time consuming and requires manual intervention with a computer screen interface, it is probably a good candidate for RPA.

How to Analyze for RPA

1. Is the process fixed and standardized? Is it mature?
2. Are there definite rules that govern the process?
3. Does it interface with a software application?
4. Are there a lot of transactions?
5. Is it a simple process?

If the volume is high and the cognitive requirements are low, it might be a candidate for RPA automation. If you can break the process into simple clear rules and humans can make errors because of volume, then it might be a candidate for RPA. Are there a lot of exceptions to the rules? Probably not a good candidate for RPA. Standard business processes like accounts payable, accounts receivable, invoicing, billing, payroll, hiring, customer service, card activation and claims processing can be good candidates. This will depend on the industry and business function. When determining if a process is a good fit for RPA both potential and relevance come into play (Leshob, et al., 2020).

RPA can replace people in the middle of systems. The "robot" can easily update the inventory system from the finance system. No people are needed. Image scanning and recognition technologies can transform documents into data. Through preset digital processes paper is transformed to data. This creates a seamless flow and automatic collection. RPA closes loops around financial issues and reporting (Yu Lian Qui and Guo Fang Xia, 2020).

RPA provides a way of looking at multidimensional cost dynamics. It can transform large amounts of messy business data into concise and up to date financial data. Back-end retrieval and calculations permit systems to talk to systems quickly. RPA can generate a cost report to meet the manager's need more quickly than humans can. It can break the data down into countless variations. Based on predetermined rules, RPA can seek the reasons for the differences between predicted and actual costs. It can provide effective cost control options and projections based on the data.

RPA is picking up steam. As RPA continues to accelerate there are a few things to keep on the radar. RPA and AI are often mistaken for each other. They are not the same thing. IPA (Intelligent Process Automation) is currently used to identify the difference. Spending on RPA is continuing to grow by double digit percentages every year. Universal adoption in the business world is inevitable. The question now is not will companies adapt and implement RPA but how effective are the RPA installations. Early on it was about getting into the game. Getting some form of RPA operational. Now, it is about RPA delivering meaningful results. The emphasis is now on evaluation not implementation. Did the RPA project deliver? Was the architecture and design what it needed to be? Did we thoroughly understand the business process we automated?

RPA will do nothing to improve a process and there are no robots involved. (Unfortunate but true). RPA Links processes together but it doesn't fix them and it is not always a perfect fit. RPA will not work as well as it could if the processes are not fully understood. Maybe RPA simply doesn't fit the process. Process mining, process discovery, process intelligence, process optimization and process orchestration are all part of the RPA vocabulary. The RPA ship has left the dock and is already headed downstream. Many companies are trying to adopt RPA without first understanding and architecting the process framework. Automation is being adopted for automation's sake. This will not endure over time.

Finance and accounting are fertile ground for RPA. They are full of repetitive, computer-based tasks and great candidates for automation. But other areas like customer experience or service are also ripe for RPA. But automating bad customer service practices will just make things worse. Before companies can improve an experience they have to totally understand the user interaction. Not what they want but what actually is.

HR is another area where RPA is exploding. HR typically has a mix of different systems. These require swivel-chair data migration throughout a worker's journey with the company. The overall hire-to-retire process can be optimized by identifying openings for automation. The expansion of RPA into HR brings new concerns about data privacy and security. The easier RPA gets to implement across systems the higher the risks.

Big data is getting bigger. RPA captures data at the interface. The variety and volume of data is increasing significantly. As RPA is linked with other technologies (IOT) this problem increases. More data allows for better insights. It also increases the chance of data leaks and security threats. Cognitive technologies like machine learning just exemplify these critical issues. Data privacy and security are critical.

RPA keeps getting better and better by greater integration among processes and systems. Process mining, RPA, AI, computer vision and machine learning are all coming together. They can complement each other. Finding ways to integrate and optimize these tools will be essential to business operations. IPA (Intelligent Process Automation) is used to describe the shift. The next step for IPA is autonomous automation. This is "bots automating processes on their own." IT teams will no longer be responsible for various apps, interfaces and database retrievals. RPA will still require human interaction and oversight. Once AI allows companies to automate the process of automation, the game changes.

Robotic Process Automation (RPA) and Intelligent Process Automation (IPA) are not the same thing. RPA is often confused with AI. Sometimes it is done intentionally and sometimes not. The two technologies are distinct. In RPA if something changes the bot will not be able to figure things out. Unlike AI, RPA bots don't have the ability to learn. RPA is designed to mimic human actions and AI is designed to simulate how humans think. IPA combines the two. It usually consists of four core technologies: RPA, Natural Language Processing (NLP), intelligent workflows and machine learning.

Natural Language Processing is software that gives computers the ability to read, understand and create meaning from words. It brings together machine learning and statistical algorithms. NLP is commonly used in chatbots and vocally activated technologies. These chatbots use RPA to communicate, determine meaning from interactions and create relevant responses.

Machine learning (ML) allows a system to access data and learn from it without being reprogrammed. ML uses algorithms to identify patterns in the data. ML can be supervised (create inputs and outputs) or unsupervised (observe data and create pattern recognition). IPA bots can adjust on their own. This improves processes. Deep learning is when the IPA can gather data in one context and use it to improve others.

Intelligent workflows are an intervention. When does a bot hand off a task to humans? Process management software helps humans and stakeholders to understand and track the flow of data. IPA helps to avoid frustration and improve customer experience.

IPA ups the game. It provides chances for humans to spend their time on tasks that offer more value to the customer. Customers also benefit from IPA. It can automate long drawn-out processes, reducing wait time and significantly improving customer experiences.

IPA can understand context, learn and iterate. It can handle data that is unstructured and support informed decision making. This can enhance task level and workflow level operations. IPA helps organizations access and analyze unstructured data like images and text to gain insights that might be important. IPA can take this data and turn it into RPA. RPA and IPA are not mutually exclusive but can work together to optimize results.

You may not be replaced by a robot... yet. You might not yet have one that cleans your house. But

RPA is here. It is quickly evolving to IPA. RPA and IPA have the potential to drastically impact the way we work. Humans need to be aware of this. They need to be ready to monitor and evaluate RPA and IPA as they penetrate our workplaces (Manning, 2020).

ASK THE HARD QUESTIONS

- Are organizations rushing to RPA too soon?
- Is anyone monitoring how effective RPA has been?
- Do we understand the processes well enough to optimize results?
- How does RPA put data security and privacy at risk?
- How does the integration of other technologies affect RPA?

Chapter 11

Intangible Assets

"If you have ideas, you have the main asset you need, and there isn't any limit to what you can do with your business and your life. Ideas are any man's greatest asset."
—Harvey S. Firestone

Businesses depend on technologies to innovate and compete. Intangible assets like intellectual property (IP), customer data and software are more important than ever. Intangibles now comprise 90% of the value of S&P 500 companies. This leaves tangibles, such as buildings, equipment and real estate making up just 10% of company value. In 1985, intangible assets made up about 35% of the value of S&P companies. According to 2018 study intangible assets represent $21 trillion. This is more than five times that of tangible assets, like real estate and equipment.

Forbes reports a silent revolution: "Over the past half century, we have witnessed a somewhat silent revolution in terms of what factors are really driving business valuations..... As the global economy has gradually shifted away from an industrial base and focuses more on services and knowledge, [we] enter the age of intangible asset, as an increasingly vital component of corporate worth" (Ali, 2021).

For years, a company's value was defined by PP&E (Property, Plant and Equipment). Lately that has been changing. An intangible asset is not physical in nature. Identifiable intangible assets can be separated from other assets and can even be sold. These are assets such as intellectual property, patents, copyrights, trademarks and trade names. Software and other computer-related assets, outside of hardware, also classify as intangible assets. Unidentifiable assets like goodwill are more difficult to pin down (Berman, 2021). PP&E worked in a different time. Now we classify these assets under intellectual property. In a knowledge-based economy, it's an attempt to bring accounting in touch with the reality of GDP.

Intangible assets reflect a much bigger mismatch. There is a difference between the value of assets and how we account for them. AI only increases the problem. It puts top management under the microscope. Digital capital and human capital produce the products and services that thrive in most developed economies. There are tangible assets like servers and routers and basic software. These appear as capital investments in a company's books. But what is even bigger and growing rapidly is a second type of asset... intangible assets. This includes all of the more subtle aspects of unique design, engaging user experiences, and digital capture of human behaviors. It includes social profiles, intense big data and algorithmic capabilities that can guide companies to growth. More intangibles include things like digital engagement and branding. Think Google and Amazon, or new business models, patents and processes licensed through AI. A large and growing part of the economy is what is now classified as an intangible asset.

The Old Way Doesn't Work

The traditional way of looking at this is to treat all of these intangible things as expenses. This means the funding is not reflected in capital because they are not company investments. Since the amounts are not amortized, they take a large bite out of reported income. Sometimes, spending on intangible assets should be treated as capital investments. They are long term not short term. Amazon's efforts to match product recommendations to your tastes or suggest video selections to Prime subscribers are more than expenses. These kinds of AI capabilities are expensive to build but they can create enduring competitive advantages.

It is important to realize these kinds of intangibles are not just the exception but the rule. Once they represented only a handful of businesses. Now the majority of the digital economy is part of the mix. Much of the spending in these digital companies is long term investment. This is particularly relevant with AI. These intangible assets can define the competitive landscape. They can affect many industries for a long time into the future.

What we need is a mind shift away from PP&E. It is time for a wake-up call. All business leaders need to embrace the importance of intangible assets. These assets can be very disruptive. Their presence is intensifying in areas like e-commerce, search, social media and behavior analytics. This is true anywhere data can be monetized. Sometimes they define new business opportunities. Sometimes they open up new markets. There are parallels between digital disruption and the industrial revolution. In the industrial revolution, engines took the place of human beings. The changes didn't come from companies investing in motors. They came from companies' understanding of how many different processes could be improved with motors and a little innovation.

Spending on digital capital represents about 30% or one-third of the GDP growth. About two-thirds of that spending is on intangible assets. Labor is more productive. There is less of it needed. All this has happened very quickly. It will continue to evolve at an increasing rate. It took 80 years for the steam engine to increase labor productivity at the same rate and about 40 for electricity. This digital revolution has happened in under 15 years. Many executives are not tuned into their organization's digital strengths and weaknesses. This results in an underinvestment in digital capital. That leads to a certainty of missed growth opportunities. Simple suggestions like restructuring data so that it is accessible to RPA and AI innovations are essential to beefing up business strategy (Bughin & Manyika, 2013).

It's about what they own and about what they don't own. Retailers that don't have access to digital behaviors may be out of business. The same thing could happen to banks or restaurants that can't access customer information. Some markets have more digital competitors. Some have fewer. Amazon for example made its mark with digital retail but it became dominant with AWS (Amazon Web Services). Organizations need to identify where they are vulnerable. How can they build digital assets quickly? Highly evolved digital algorithms at Netflix allows them to recommend things to viewers that cable companies never could. That is an intangible asset.

Intangible assets also affect how companies use third parties and how they engage in tech partnerships. Are you in bed with partners that are outdated? Who's leading who? Is the technology running the company or is the company running the technology?

Intellectual Capital

There is no question that decision-making is more dependent now than ever on the strength of intangible assets. These intangible assets help to increase competitive advantages and add value. The word intangible comes from the Latin word tangere or touches. They are assets that cannot be touched because they have no body. This brings up the question of people and innovation. People care about tangible but the innovation they inspire and deliver on is not. The digital age has given us a world that is made of information and data. It is more important than any other resource. It is the raw material of innovation and the decision-making process. Intangible assets are long term competitive advantages for companies and even industry sectors (Bughin & Manyika, 2021).

We used to say "the gold is in the data" but intangible assets have changed all that. Data alone is of little use to organizations. Information is now the key. Information is formed from the data but is more than just data. It is intended to change the way a customer, client or recipient sees something. It impacts their behaviors and decisions. Intellectual capital is a term used to describe the sum total of all the collective knowledge in a company. Intellectual capital is an intangible asset. In order for intellectual capital to benefit the company, it is better if it is systematized. This prevents loss when people leave and/or when they go to work for the competition.

Human beings make up the market. They create the demand for company products and services. In order for organizations to survive they have to offer goods and services to a market. They need to have processes and structures to meet human demand. Everything starts with humans. It may go through processes that involve humans and/or AI and then return something back to humans. Intangible assets are created to ultimately serve humans, inside or outside of the company. The processes are there to serve humans, not the other way around. Some examples of processes that can become intangible assets are access to information systems, alignment of human resources strategy, learning and development pathways, copyrights, competitive intelligence, networks of organizational relationships, waste reduction and sustainability, and employee satisfaction.

AI Intangible Assets

What AI does is allow machines to create intangible assets by structuring and accelerating process controls. Examples of this include research and development, communications, computerization, information processing, operations, performance evaluations, operational processes and flows. Other examples are customer service, monitoring, systematic control, building goals and implementing strategies.

There are many ways to categorize and group intangible assets. These four are usually used: human capital, customer capital, organizational capital and intellectual capital.

Human capital is a term coined by the U.S. government. It is used to describe skills and procedures attributed to humans that impact business. It is the economic value of the workers' skills and experience. Employers can improve human capital by investing in training, education and other benefits for their employees. HR is usually in charge of human capital. There is a correlation between investment and value. Human capital does not appear on the balance sheet as an intangible asset. It has become more valuable in a knowledge-based economy. Human capital can depreciate if the company doesn't keep up with technologies or if the company doesn't have the ability to innovate. The term Human Capital can be traced back to Adam Smith in *The Wealth of Nations*. He referred to investing in education and training. He said it was a win-win for everyone. Other economists use the term for the human aspects of improving production either in manufacturing or in technologies. These ideas are often criticized for making workers and people into capitalists.

Customer capital describes the relationships companies have with their customers. This includes the value customers place on the company and on increased customer solutions. Customer capital is an advantage. Companies can produce a particular good or service at a lower opportunity cost than other companies trying for the same market. These theories can be traced back to the mid-1800s. Customer capital is intangible. It can include relationships with workers and customers. It can also include franchises, licenses and trademarks. Customer capital is anything that influences customer relationships.

Organizational capital is a company's ability to compose knowledge. It can include intellectual property such as databases, code, patents, proprietary processes, trademarks, software and more. It can also include business processes, shared culture, values and anything intangible that gives it an edge over the competition.

Intellectual capital is also a relatively new term. It is detailed in a 2002 article written by Paolo Magrassi, titled "A Taxonomy of Intellectual Capital." He defines human capital as "the knowledge and competencies residing with the company's employees." He defines organizational intellectual capital as "the collective know-how, even beyond the capabilities of individual employees, that contributes to an organization." Either by layoffs, retirement or attrition, much intellectual capital within an organization is lost. Until recently, it was not possible or a priority to capture this within an organization. In "The Gig Economy," workers are less loyal and more mobile. Knowledge is lost when workers leave. Their skills are not passed along to others (Rojo et al., 2020).

Think about the logo for Apple. There is no question that intangible assets add value to an organization. The challenge is how to measure it. The grouping of intangible assets can vary greatly. Systematic collection and storage of data, management of processes and production control can be groups of assets. So can images, trademarks and patents that help promote the company's market presence. Market Value Added is used because it correlates to the value of the company's shares. Without getting into financial statements, it is key to remember that innovations like AI integration can directly impact financial stability. There are many terms and no one definition for intangible assets. The question is how to evaluate more and more companies with a growing focus on intangible assets.

Companies are spending more on intangible assets. Studies show there is a correlation between intangible investing and growth. This is true regardless of industry sector. Investments in intangible assets are increasing in technology, healthcare, manufacturing, financial services, telecommunications, media and retail. There is a shift towards an economy based not on things but on knowledge. Eric Hazen from McKinsey said, "In the 19th century, the tools of growth were industrial machines; the tools of the knowledge economy will be intangible assets. We could well be seeing a new stage in the history of capitalism based on learning, knowledge, and intellectual capital" (Poerter, 2021).

Digital Platforms

Investments in technology will be repositioned from an expense to an investment in the future. Everything needs to be able to be scaled and monetized. Looking forward more than five or ten years is almost impossible with intangible assets. Certainly, platforms and algorithms are key to this expansion. Digital platforms are rapidly becoming the leading business model for the 21st century. They are essential for building intangible assets. In addition to driving revenue, platforms draw in more customers. They spin off more data and create new data opportunities. These can become intangible assets in other areas. A platform is essentially a multi-sided marketplace that connects parties on each side. Its network effects create a magnetic circle that attracts ever more producers and consumers to the platform. This connection is enabled by the digital world. It empowers platforms from the individual level all the way up to global.

Couple platforms with algorithms and it's a game changer. An algorithm is a set of rules for solving a problem. They use a finite number of steps and when computerized bring greater consistency to the findings. Computers can use large amounts of data and can increase the speed of decision making. In the intangible economy, algorithms will be one of the most valuable assets. ML and AI algorithms allow computers to create their own rules. This progressively improves the decision-making process. Algorithms, especially using ML and AI, need to be monitored. Someone needs to be watching the shop. An AI Auditor monitors the findings. The auditor works with managers and builders to understand the performance of the algorithm, bias and all. Bias is a normal part of algorithms. Knowing what the bias is and how it influences results requires understanding both how a model works and how individual decisions are made. Critical too are metrics for the performance of algorithms and the impact on business objectives. Data is at the heart of all this. Any time there is data involved, questions about privacy, regulation and compliance are too (Rimmer, 2019).

Intellectual property is one of the most valuable assets on the planet. Innovation and the pace companies create new intangible assets is their competitive advantage. Intangible assets are hard to manage, define and value. They make up more of the S&P 500 value than anything else. Traditional metrics aren't working with the explosion of this new assets class. Patents, copyrights, training, algorithms and platforms hold a place in organizational success. This wasn't even imaginable a few decades ago. Understanding and determining the value of intangible assets is difficult. It is also difficult to determine costs for maintaining them. Metrics usually refers to quantity. Quantity just doesn't cut it with this asset class. Companies make the decision to ramp up digitization and invest in intangible assets, but it isn't easy. It can be a long and expensive road to execute the strategies.

There is a paradigm shift. AI and intangible assets are fostering a new level of understanding about what will be rewarded. Understanding a company's internal position with intangible assets and then the competitions' is daunting. The transformation is coming by changing perspective from Man vs. Machine to Man + Machine. The challenge is to combine computer and AI power with human understanding. This requires everyone to up their game. Organizations are beginning to realize that to compete they have to have AI. Many companies have experimented with AI on a small scale. Maybe it's a chatbot in customer service or a bot in HR. Intangible assets open up new efficiencies and increase productivity.

Across the enterprise, new outcomes are possible with AI as an asset. The challenge is to develop strategies that empower everyone and every process. Intangible assets need to be scalable. Then AI services can help achieve business objectives faster. Thanks to the cloud, increased computing power and connection, AI is getting easier. With the huge boost in data access AI can be created, managed and controlled. To reduce operating costs, improve the margin, scale personalized experiences, or create completely new revenue streams, companies profit from speed. Speed is a universal indicator of success in a world that moves more quickly every day. AI is what will make that possible.

ASK THE HARD QUESTIONS

- What two new streams of knowledge might change your business?
- How might intangible assets change your business culture? Heritage?
- Do businesses understand economics or accounting better? Which one influences intangible assets? How are they different?
- What creates value for you personally? For your organization?
- Is intellectual capital an intangible asset? How does AI figure into intellectual capital?

Chapter 12

Uncoded Bias in AI

"AI doesn't have to be evil to destroy humanity – if AI has a goal and humanity just happens to come in the way, it will destroy humanity as a matter of course without even thinking about it, no hard feelings."
—Elon Musk

The workforce creating AI is mostly white men. The thinking is pretty clear that AI is going to play a big part in the future of work. It will be a part of search engines, data lakes, email and autonomous vehicles. It will help police protect us and the military fight our enemies. It will help doctors treat patients and diagnose disease and help us to create vaccines to fight them off. Big Tech is building it and building in the biases that this mostly white male society may already have, conscious or unconscious.

The improvements rocking the workplace are increasing in intensity and effect. It is moving in leaps and bounds. Big changes and fast changes. Bias is part of the progress and bias is something that tech companies don't want to own. Dr. Timnit Gebru of Stanford University put it like this: "I'm not worried about machines taking over the world. I'm worried about group think, insularity and arrogance in the AI community – especially with the current hype and demand for people in the field" (Metz, 2021). She also raises the question that if a few are creating it and those few represent a big part of the system, who will benefit? A few? Who will it harm? Many.

Is this where humanity wants to go? There are other stories too. Stories about bias against black people, not recognizing them without a white mask, and AI systems categorizing blacks as gorillas. She used to work for Google but now she doesn't. Her boss used to work for Google and she's gone now too. She defended Dr. Gebru. Facial recognition, chatbots and talking assistants rely on AI. The problem with AI is that through neural networks it grows – on its own with no further intervention from humans. AI gets trained by analyzing lots of data. In the cases of miscataloging pictures, it was pictures of gorillas. How did Google fix it? They eliminated the category of gorillas in Google Photo. In the case of white masks, the training had been done with mostly white and mostly male people's photos. The AI could recognize faces that were white because that's how it had been trained. The data AI uses matters. In fact, it is critical. Police departments, the military and courts are using AI for identification, and this can impact human rights. It's not just Google. Amazon and Microsoft have had issues too. There is little government regulation and few restrictions on use.

Putting Big Tech in charge of regulating itself is putting the fox in charge of the hen house. We live in a capitalist society set on making profits. Facebook is an organization that values more connection at all costs. Even if that connection is based on lies. This resulted in AI supporting the spread of "fake news." On Google's search engine it is the bias built in against women and blacks. Tech is supposed to regulate tech. With AI the stakes are just too high. You don't have to look far to find areas where AI has already crept into humanity. Uncoded bias has found its way into advertising, social media, human resources. Just about every other application that expounds the use of AI has bias. Computers are not capable of seeing things that are not measured. AI's ability to make sense out of that data is limited to the data itself. Systems can only change their approach to analyzing and making knowledge out of data by recoding. They can't figure it out on their own. So, although computers can address some incidental cases of uncoded bias, most of it is left unchecked.

Data Wears Out

Even non-analytic-oriented people tend to understand the idea of regression to the mean. It's the tendency for a measurement to reproduce itself. It's how data wears itself out. It kills off variability once it discovers it and eventually this leads to average and static. So, although everyone wants to obtain certain performance goals, data models are rarely built to push the limits. They don't go beyond those goals. What data models are great at is producing predictable results. What they are not very good at is delivering meaningful results to a constantly changing target. This tendency pretty much destroys the ideas of constant improvement and innovation. Once they stop creating new value, what's the point? The real issue here is not what is known but what remains unknown. The things that we don't know, we don't know, unknown unknowns.

Human decisions are capable of being open to unforeseen variables. Not so with computer algorithms. There is always a bias towards reaching the goal. They are focused on the target and that doesn't allow them to see unforeseen circumstances. An example of this is our understanding of the degree that our biases impact opportunities for protected classes. There is a great deal of work to be done on providing opportunities to all people. This is part of our journey toward diversity, equity and inclusion. It is a destination which still has many unknowns as we attempt to move forward. Unconscious bias has to be examined and reexamined. It has to be brought to light and addressed. What is true for organizations is also true for machine algorithms: Bias has to be addressed.

Good Intentions

A great example of good intentions gone off track is Open AI's GPT-3. It is an artificial intelligence model that can write poetry, news articles and programming code. Soon after it was launch it was discovered that GPT-3 was being used to generate child pornography. It also had a distinct bias against Muslims. Once again the tech biz was scrambling to constrain the dark side of AI. There is no doubt that this technology is moving rapidly but maybe too rapidly, if it is spreading disinformation and perpetuating biases. Big language models have become vogue in the AI world. Researchers are scrambling to understand exactly where they succeed, how they fall short and what has to be improved. Unregulated, hate speech has appeared to generate more of the same. Unless it is labeled as unsafe, by humans, AI remains untrained. GPT-3 has an impressive readability and can understand and create language. It can take the SATs with better results than most people. It has fooled Reddit users and remained anonymous. But its creators knew, before it was licensed to developers, it might generate racism and sexism. Academia has issued many warnings on how studies on large language models might be misused. They can adversely affect prejudice and bias in society. Large AI is more likely to engage in stereotyping. These models grow more toxic as they get bigger and bigger. Probably because of regression to the mean (Simonite, 2021).

Gender bias is another example. AI will displace more women than men and force them to make occupational transitions because of the nature of their work. Their current occupations will change. In order to stay employed they will need to find new kinds of jobs. A very large number of women are going to need to learn to work with technology. Their current jobs are going to require them to interface with applications and use AI to do some kind of analysis. It doesn't matter if you are a nurse in a hospital or a financial advisor at a bank, these kinds of jobs will require new skill sets. It is critical that the impact of AI on women in the workplace is clearly understood. If sexism is part of the data, then AI will pick that up and apply it to its output. The workforce that builds AI is predominantly male. If males are unconsciously adding their bias to the algorithms, they are creating new rules. Human beings are not free of biases. How much intelligence is in the algorithm to rectify bias? How is farness defined?

Fair and Transparent

Is fairness defined as what a human would have decided without the inclusion of AI? Human decision track records in the past have not been stellar. One of AI's missions is to make better decisions than humans have in the past and de-bias the decision-making process. Again, it's all back to the data. Test data and real-world data can be very different. This can result in bias being amplified. AI has been treated like a black box. No transparency and very little oversight, up until now.

A perfect example is Google Translate. If you put in two sentences: "She's president. He's cooking" into a gender-neutral language like Turkish they become "This person is president. This person is cooking." If you ask Google Translate to translate them back and provide a gender it will come back: "He's president. She's cooking." That's gender bias in action. This is a simple and small-scale example but there are also bigger fish in the sea. There is bias in data because of the data itself. The medical system is a perfect example. Many medicines are tested on men and only men. This creates gaps in the data because of things that happen in ordinary life. Siri and Amazon's Alexa have women's voices because they are giving the psychological impact of being submissive and obliging, someone that follows orders. And when things screw up, the female voice is the face of that failure. This is not accidental. Humans have a responsibility in the design to address bias and fairness. AI is being used everywhere to screen employees and provide access to schools. AI algorithms can look at data, facial recognition, images and verbal and nonverbal cues.

The point of all this is transparency. There is a strong need to make these algorithms more transparent to the people who use them and rely on their decision-making prowess. This is critical because AI has tremendous potential for good as well as darkness. HR is an area where AI has tremendous potential. AI can assess cognitive and personality traits and determine if a person is a good match for a certain role or position. They can compare profiles of top performers in certain roles and then match candidates to those profiles. Often these traits are based on people who are currently in those roles. Which can have its own problems. What is important is the ability to audit AI and keep control of the ultimate impact on people and the organization's needs. In a way AI has done us a great favor by mirroring the bias that is currently in our workplace and society as a whole. It brings up a certain awareness of the kind of mind shift that needs to happen.

There is a diversity emergency in AI around gender and race. As I said before, bias has also shown up as racism. There's the story of a black researcher in Boston who found that an AI program could not recognize her face unless she put on a white mask.

As mentioned previously Google Photos was capable of categorizing black faces as gorillas. It was because of a simple mistake in tagging 80 photos. Then the neural network grew from there. It was capable of reviewing and categorizing thousands of photos of gorillas, and it was also capable of making terrible mistakes. The fix was for Google Photos to stop using "gorilla" as a photo category. Similar examples have shown up with facial recognition. Facial recognition systems have been proven to have issues recognizing black faces. This problem is probably exemplified because the majority of faces used to train it were white and male (Metz, 2021).

A good place to start might be with more women in Big Tech, which has traditionally been a male dominated field. AI algorithms project female stereotypes because little female input was involved. Having more women in the room will lead to more equity. The culture will change when the mix of contributors change. The impact will be reflected in organizations and eventually in society as a whole (McKinsey, 2021). Research shows that only 18% of all authors at leading AI conferences are women. 80% of AI professors are men. The AI workforce is even worse. Women comprise only 15% of the workforce at Facebook and 10% at Google. Black workers have an even deeper gap. Only 2.5% of Google's workforce and 4% of Facebook's and Microsoft's workforce are black. What is probably the most troubling is that the industry is having trouble recognizing and addressing the diversity problem. They failed to admit there is an unequal distribution of power. This has resulted in AI reinforcing inequalities. Bias in AI tends to reflect historical patterns of discrimination in our society. The two are not separate and must be addressed together. The vast majority of AI studies assume gender is binary. They erase all other forms of gender identity. Using AI in any area that involves the classification, detection and prediction of race and gender needs to be evaluated and soon.

Race and gender classification based on appearance or language can be flawed at best. It can be easily abused. AI systems using photos or physical appearance are a case in point. Micro expressions, sexuality and criminality are all being predicted based on headshots. The commercial sale and development of any AI tools needs to be closely regulated and monitored. The challenge is most AI systems are opaque. Transparency is essential. It is important to be open about who is using AI and what purpose it is being used for. This is the tip of the iceberg. Unraveling bias in AI has to go beyond technical issues. It needs to include how AI is being used in context. Prerelease trials, monitoring and independent audits are essential. We need to test for bias, discrimination and other harmful effects. This includes asking bigger questions. We need to expand assessments of certain systems and ask hard questions. Then conduct detailed risk assessments. Then make human and moral decisions on whether AI should be developed and used at all.

AI by its very nature is discriminatory. It's a system that sorts, classifies, analyzes and ranks in order to differentiate. There is a growing call for ethical AI and not just fairness as defined mathematically. The AI industry should stop keeping secrets. It needs to publish results of discrimination and bias. This includes the number and details of claims and lawsuits. Committing to transparency in areas like hiring, promotion, salaries and turnover is also important. The diversity problem is not just about women or race in AI. It's about power. Power determines what products get built. It determines who they are designed to serve and who benefits from their development.

AI bias is not a simple concept. It is not just about regression to the mean. It is about expanding beyond the technologies. It is about looking at not only how AI can be biased technology but how these tools are shaped by the environment they're built in and the people that build them.

GAN (Generative Adversarial Network) is a good example of this. A GAN is a class of machine learning developed by Ian Goodfellow and colleagues in 2014. Given a training set of data, GAN can generate new data with the same statistics as the original training set of data. A GAN trained on photographs can generate photographs that have many realistic characteristics. These programs are zero sum and generative and unsupervised. GAN has proved useful when semi-supervised, supervised or used for reinforcement learning. They can be used to generate art, change photographs, for interior design, for industrial design and in video games. They have also been used to generate "deep fakes."

At the heart of AI is a super-challenging question. Since all models and algorithms drift (wear out) maintenance is a part of keeping them up to speed. Who is doing the maintenance? Designers like to create not maintain. Unlike the excitement and glory of product development, maintenance is done to manage risk, and restore, refurbish and create incremental improvements. AI designs that do not include maintenance are not sustainable.

Can the team that comes after the initial design crew, either internally or externally, make sense of the original setup, the models? Logic and decisions? Generally, this is not part of the current conversation. AI is all about learning. It is constantly changing. The problem is it is very difficult to tell how far the intelligent tools have drifted (HR Examiner, 2021). Facebook is a perfect example.

Who's in Charge?

Part of the challenge of the current state of AI is people don't understand the AI software. It can't explain itself. Artificial Intelligence has transformed everything from drug discovery to package delivery. The powerful ability to analyze and identify patterns in data is increasing. It is complex. It is this complexity that allows modern deep-learning networks to successfully teach themselves. Even AI experts have problems identifying the inner workings because they are applied to black box ideas like driving cars and insurance fraud. The knowledge is spread across many layers of computer neurons. Each with hundreds of thousands of connections. It's for all intents and purposes a black box.

Why is this so critical? Because we are in the beginning of something that can change being human forever. We are in the critical stage of deciding whether this technology is good or bad for human beings. If we can figure this out we might not move forward with this revolution. It's very difficult and risky to have confidence in a system when you don't understand how it works. The real question is can we grow to openly understand AI so we can effectively use it? Can we confirm it is safe and that knowledge about it is available?

The AI sector needs a big change in how it handles diversity and inclusion. So far there has been no substantial progress in diversity including assuming gender is binary. Workplace cultures, power issues, harassment and exclusionary hiring plus unfair compensation and tokenization are causing people to leave or avoid employment in AI. Academic workplaces need to ensure greater diversity in all spaces where AI research is conducted. The AI sector needs to be more transparent in their hiring practices. This includes publishing compensation, bonuses, roles and job categories by race and gender. They need to commit to transparency in hiring practices. They need to publish harassment claims submitted and actions taken. They need to make a concerted effort to hire more women and people of color in leadership roles. And they need to ensure that the incentive structure is tied to increases in hiring and retaining underrepresented groups.

Transparency is also the key to AI bias in the systems themselves. The field of bias and fairness needs to go beyond technical debiasing. It should include a wider social context of how AI is being used. This includes assessments of whether certain AI systems should be designed at all. This must be based on risk assessment. Discrimination in AI, both in business and academic circles, affects who builds products and what products get build. It also effects who benefits from the development (West, et al., 2019).

AI should reflect human morals and knowledge. The ethics and privacy of the models is very important to their use. If doctors are trying to diagnose cancer, for example, they might look at fused glands, prior chemo treatments, age and other defined factors. These are concepts that are definable and are what human doctors might care about. If the AI program can show that this is what it is looking at, it is reflecting human understanding and is more understandable itself. Humans communicate with concepts not 1s and 0s. That's fine for computers but not human beings (Quanta Magazine, 2021).

We also need to remember models are only abstract representations of some process, nothing more. If they update they are usually looked at as a dynamic model. They are still quite limited. The model asks the questions we want it to ask. It collects the data we want it to collect. Our own values and opinions influence how we create models. They are influenced by who created them and what the company or organization is trying to accomplish. The big question is whether they eliminate bias or just cover it up with mathematics (O'Neil, 2017).

This brings us back to the question of understanding the algorithms and transparency of what they are doing and why. Algorithms by design are "black boxes." The claim is that they are intellectual property and top secret. They are the "secret sauce" of giants like Google, Facebook and Amazon. They are worth billions or more. It is the size and reach of these kinds of mathematical models that can turn little problems in to devastatingly destructive ones. The size, opacity and scale of these models can turn nuisances in to tsunami forces. Mathematical models are based on the past and on assumptions of the predictable patterns repeating. Many of these models are developed to manipulate, control and intimidate people. Transparency matters and an awareness and respect for human privacy and ethics is vital.

ASK THE HARD QUESTIONS

- How do workforces and AI interact? Who is in the loop?

- Are AI systems by nature systems of discrimination? Do they classify, differentiate, rank and categorize?

- Where do you find disparity in hiring? Promotion? Biased stereotypes? Biological Determinism?

- Since AI is finding its way into all aspects of our lives, is it important to assess how AI treats people differently? In healthcare? Education? Safety? Opportunities?

- Should AI include both social and ethical approaches to support more equity?

Chapter 13

Privacy and Ethics

"The real question is when will we draft an artificial intelligence bill of rights? What will it consist of? And who will get to decide that?"
—Gray Scott

The Fourth Amendment of the United States Constitution guarantees protection against unreasonable search and seizure. It was written when everything was paper and ink and messages were delivered on horseback. We live in the digital age. This amendment has been interpreted in ways that diminish our rights. Our most important communications come to us digitally. Companies like Google, AT&T, Facebook, Instagram, Twitter, LinkedIn and Tik-Tok hold our metadata. They know who we talk to and when. They also know where we are. They know what we watch and read. Now it's time to align the Fourth Amendment with modern life in the digital age. It's time we use technology, data and systems in a fair and ethical way. Realigning the Fourth Amendment is a great place to start (Cohn, 2021).

Whatever happened to privacy protection? Even your face is not your own. The app Clearview was created by simply scraping the public web—Facebook, YouTube, Venmo, employment sites and other social media—to create a database for facial recognition that contained three billion images of people. With Clearview it was effortless to go from a face to a Facebook account. At first only law enforcement knew about it but that didn't last long. The big social media players sent cease and desist letters to the company. They were basically ignored. Legal threats have begun to move through the courts, but so far not much has happened. The majority of us post pictures next to our names all the time. Illinois is the only state that has a law, the Biometric Information Privacy Act (BIPA) that protects people's faces. As technology advanced, policy makers didn't keep up. Privacy became compromised. In Illinois you must grant permission to a company to use your biometric or they can be fined up to $5,000. In 2020

Facebook settled a suit with them for $650 million. Clearview is now fighting 13 lawsuits from Illinois (Hill, 2021).

In China facial recognition aids in enforcing the law and surveilling the population. It is a social norm. It's been used to shame people for wearing their pajamas in public and flagging minorities like the Uighurs and tracking their comings and goings. In the U.S. it is a little more curtailed by both laws and norms than in Russia and China. It is impossible to tell how technology will ultimately impact human privacy and will change our world.

On a day that will go down in history, January 6, 2021, the U.S. Capitol Riots put Clearview to use. Although the FBI will not confirm it, the app was probably being used to track down the rioters. Suddenly things changed. It seems that privacy depends on context. With people storming the capitol, privacy seemed different. Detractors tend to change their mind when the technology is applied to a different use case. What are the limits? Where is this going? No one really knows.

Privacy and Surveillance

It's not just Alexa recording your every word or Siri or Cortana, even your grocery store may be wired to track your every move. They use a tool called Bluetooth Beacons to determine your exact location. They are hidden throughout the grocery store. They can tell if you are in the dairy or cereal aisle. They can send you coupons and bonuses via their app or your text message. Bluetooth Beacons are watching you using technology that is already in your phone. Companies want to know how to monetize your habits both online and off. The only way they can know that is through tracking and surveillance. Many companies defend the practice by stating that micro data collection is a choice. You can opt out of location services. But most people don't even know what a Beacon is let alone how to opt out. There is also the issue on who is using the Beacons and for what. Target could let a third party use its Beacons to collect data on you for a fee. Apple and Google are tracking you through iOS and Android, but their methods are not transparent. There is really no easy way to tell if you are being tracked by a Beacon. There is also no easy way to know which apps on your phone have Beacon tracking and which do not (Kwet, 2019).

In order to create, perfect and train AI the major players have resorted to using cheap contract labor to listen in on device-recorded conversations. In the fall of 2014, about the time Amazon came out with the Echo speaker featuring Alexa, a contractor reported listening to clips of people's intimate moments recorded in their homes. She was paid $12 an hour. Her name was Ruthy Hope Slatis. Amazon was capturing voice commands in the Cloud and relying on workers like Ruthy to train their system. The contractor program grew along with Alexa's popularity. Were the people told they were being recorded and listened to by other human beings? Did they understand that? Probably or most definitely not. Over 100 million Amazon devices have been purchased as of 2019. That's about one for every person on earth. The mics in kitchens and bedrooms are always on. It's a creepy loss of privacy that just keeps evolving. People don't know how to protect themselves and don't know that they should. Amazon retains the recordings indefinitely. No one is really sure where or why.

Why Privacy is Everything

Apple, Amazon and Facebook are all guilty of using humans to review other humans' conversations without their knowledge. Contractors sign a non-disclosure agreement and fear reprisals. And then they leave. Turnover is very high because for most of them it just doesn't feel right. Apple is becoming more aggressive since Siri isn't the only game in town. They fear she is falling behind Alexa, which has 70% of the market. Training on privacy issues is minimal. The contractors are expected to transcribe every clip that comes in. By 2015 Apple's machines were processing more than a billion requests a week. The devices are always listening. Apple has nothing to say. They still don't see the system in place as a violation of privacy. By 2019 Siri was on more devices and Apple was processing over 19 billion voice commands a month.

As AI grew and more recording came in, the companies began to recruit transcribers overseas. Microsoft admits to using humans to review voice data registered through its voice recognition system in Cortana. Google Assistant feeds its search engine with queries from a billion devices, including Android smart phones, tablets, Nest thermometers and Google TV. Facebook has had its own issues. They didn't end with the Cambridge Analytica mess. Facebook relies on human transcribers for its Messenger app which allows audio not just texting. Although all of the big players have cleaned up their act a little, this is a well-established and accepted thing in the AI industry. It remains unregulated for the most part. This includes listening to children. It's easy to see how an authoritarian government or a corrupt agency could take advantage of these pervasive surveillance networks. There is talk about change but the people with the authority to enact change are moving very slowly (Carr, et al., 2019).

AI has also crept into Human Resource departments. It can analyze, predict and diagnose applications. It makes processing transactions quicker. AI can be found in recruiting, training, onboarding, performance analysis and retention. In 2019, Oracle reported that employees would trust the advice of a robot over their manager 64% of the time. Research also shows that about 65% of the employees studied felt good about this. Companies are investing in AI for HR because it saves them money and time. Much of what HR traditionally does is repetitive, tedious tasks like reentering new applicants' information over and over again. Many companies are using AI to assess candidates before they talk to a recruiter. AI is also being used to analyze performance data including referrals. In theory AI can help HR focus on strategic and creative work. It can free them up from repetitive and low value tasks. Companies are working on capturing everything possible through the employee's life cycle, so they can improve engagement and retention. Turnover costs money.

Chatbots talk with employees on a daily basis. The conversations are personal. They are then analyzed and leveraged to address specific concerns and employee wants and needs. The idea is to understand sentiment so that managers can prove to employees their voices make a difference. They also have another angle. They use these data analytics to show the impact on the business.

The Agile workplace demands agile learning models. Learning and Development has to teach people AI skills and also adapt to changes. Agile learning supports the individual when and where it is needed. Agile learning is personal learning. It is based on a person's job role, existing skills, future goals and developing a plan to fill in the skill gaps. AI helps with content matching and cross functional projects. Agile means relevant to individual employee's availability and needs. Chatbot access in real time takes care of frequently asked questions. It gets employees answers quickly. AI can show managers the impact of shift changes, time off and unplanned schedule changes. AI is reaching mainstream rapidly. The relationship between humans and machines is being redefined in the workplace.

There is no question that new technologies like artificial intelligence, the Internet of Things, and augmented/virtual reality are changing the way we work. RPA automates repetitive tasks and AI helps to automate human tasks on a larger scale. AI can protect, read and classify personal information on a scale that was beyond our wildest dreams just a few decades ago. It can give workers the right information, at the right time, to get work done. The most important aspect of this is "scale." AI can help organizations scale access to data. Remember that scale rather than complexity is key. Humans can do really complex work, but they don't scale well. AI is just the opposite. AI is reinventing HR by pushing back on paper pushing. The COVID pandemic thrust us into hybrid work and learning. Many of these systems have a form of AI incorporated. They allow for real time transcription services and recording meetings and notes. Many of these systems monitor the audio and reactions on the video. Call centers use verbal and onscreen interaction with artificial intelligence to guide agents on how to properly handle inbound and outbound calls (Nicastro, 2021).

McDonald's is being sued because of its lack of respect for Illinois privacy laws. Apparently the McDonald's drive in bot is less than charming. Of course, they are using a "female" voice. It is also recording voice prints of the customers at the drive in. Illinois is one of only 12 states that requires both parties to consent to recording a voice conversation. A lawsuit claims that there is no warning to the customer that the recording will happen. In another big move, McDonald's partnered with IBM so that Watson can collect data and personalize your experience. Both companies insist that they are committed to transparency. They embed ethical principles into AI applications to build trust. But we've heard this before, right? (Matyszczyk, 2021).

Western societies are built on the premise of privacy. We put ourselves rather than the government in control. The idea is that individuals know what quality is to their lives and they and they alone have the power to determine what that is. AI has the power to change all this. There is a danger in letting others know more about ourselves than we do. AI could lead us to totalitarianism. Freedom will be obedience to the state. China is a perfect example of how this technology can be misused. The Chinese communist party-state is using AI to develop a "citizen score" to incentivize good behavior according to their standards. This AI spying is a threat to civil liberties in a country that is already one of the most oppressive and controlling in the world (Mitchell and Diamond, 2018).

AI is only going to improve and, as Yuval Noah Harari suggests in *21 Lessons for the 21st Century*, it may tell us who we are before we know ourselves. This fact has universal, personal and political implications. The Russian Communist leader Lenin said that capitalists would sell him the tool that would hang them. Perhaps he was right. Silicon Valley has sold communism a tool that threatens to bring down democracy by destroying privacy. It has the potential to undermine democratic society. There is a power gap with evolving AI. It is between what we know about ourselves and what knowledge lies in someone's hands that has power over us. There needs to be a change in ideology towards nothing about us without us knowing it. What AI tells us about ourselves is for us to use. Not for others to abuse.

Fired by an Algorithm

Well, it's happened to truck drivers and teachers alike. A 63-year-old Army veteran in Phoenix, AZ was fired by an automated email created by a bot. The bot suspected he wasn't doing his job properly after four years with the company. Amazon became who they are today by outsourcing its sprawling operations to algorithms. These sets of computer instructions are designed to solve problems. Four other drivers and managers who were fired say the algorithmic system isn't attuned to the real-life challenges faced by drivers. Amazon operates a GIG driver service called Amazon Flex Driver, which recruits an army of contract drivers. Amazon knew there would be problems but decided to trust the Flex algorithms. It was cheaper than investigating mistaken firings. Drivers are easy to find.

Amazons said it worked hard to make the algorithm fair. It considered delays and traffic jams. Because of Amazon's size even a small margin of error can be considered a huge success for the company, even if it causes a lot of pain and financial loss for the drivers. Here is a copy of one of the email exchanges between the human and the bot that went on with Amazon. The man was fired on October 2, 2020:

I have met standards and exceeded standards for over 3.5 years now and never had any problems up until I started working out of SAZ1/VAZ1 some late deliveries and one issue back on Aug 24 due to hub malfunction and access to apts.

THIS HAS TO BE A MISTAKE! I depend on this to survive.

Just what standards have I not met? This email is not specific.

I have documented everything and had contact with driver support many times about any issues on late deliveries which is really the only issues I've ever had. I have a consistent rating of always getting everything delivered, I have never missed a block I always show up on time (early) and I've never canceled late this just doesn't make any sense. This just has to be a mistake and should be resolved immediately. I am very upset and I will take this to escalation immediately.

Stephen Normandin

Sent from AOL Mobile Mail

Here is the response:

-----Original Message-----

From: Amazon.com

To: ▇▇▇▇▇▇▇

Sent: Sat, Oct 3, 2020 12:08 pm

Subject: A Message from Amazon Flex Support

Hello Stephen, Thank you for providing us with more context about your history with Amazon Flex. We'll consider this information and your eligibility to continue participating in the Amazon Flex program. We will reach out to you with a response within the next six days. Thank you for your patience.

We'd appreciate your feedback. Please use the buttons below to vote about your experience today.

Regards, Bitan Banerjee

The Amazon Flex Team

After a host of email exchanges with Amazon, on October 28 the man received his final walking papers from "SYAM," which stated they understood things could be difficult, but they had already taken that into consideration. He wasn't getting his job back (Soper, 2022).

So far Amazon hasn't had much trouble hiring drivers. Millions have downloaded their app. Internally at Amazon, it is considered a huge success. Amazon insists it has invested heavily in the Flex program and that it's working. As contractors, many drivers have little or no recourse if they are terminated without a good reason. Many just leave because they don't believe they can meet the demands of the algorithm. Demands like driving on snowy roads in winter with the promise of a two-hour delivery time. They can go to arbitration for a cost, but most don't bother.

There is another case of a woman driver who had delivered 8,000 packages for Amazon. She got an email one day saying she was an excellent driver. The next day it said she was no longer eligible for Flex. After several appeals and emails back and forth with something or someone, she was told that they were sticking to their original decision. The truth is that neither Amazon nor the algorithm has any idea about the obstacles that a driver must face delivering packages. The big challenge is knowing if you are communicating with machines or real people. Most of the time drivers don't know. The inside sentiments are "Amazon just doesn't care," they know everyone will get their package sooner or later and most folks will get it on time.

Amazon has also automated their HR department more than most companies. Using algorithms that make decisions affecting human lives is increasingly common. AI is used for loan approval and credit ratings. It is used to decide who stays behind bars and who deserves parole. AI has found its way into very intricate human situations. Many experts have demanded that companies be more transparent with how their algorithms affect people. Law makers have been doing the same thing but have been very slow to act. Some legislatures have tried to create certain rules that ensure algorithms are being used equitably and those affected by decisions are able to reverse mistakes. So far this has gone nowhere.

Human Oversight

Algorithms set up police patrols, prison sentences and probation rules. Algorithms can now grant parole or take it away. The big question is where is the human oversight? In Philadelphia, an algorithm created by a professor at the University of Pennsylvania dictates probation. It's only one of many. Algorithms are used to make decisions about people's lives both in the United States and Europe. Nearly every U.S. state uses some kind of governance algorithm. This is according to the Electronic Privacy Information Center. Algorithm Watch is a counterpart in Europe. They have discovered similar technologies in sixteen European countries. United Nation lawyers, civil rights lawyers, labor organizers and community groups are pushing back. There is little or no transparency in how these decisions are made. People are angry about the growing number of machines being used to make critical life-changing decisions. They are taking humans and transparency out of the equation.

Predictive algorithms use historical data to calculate the probabilities of future events. It is very similar to the way sports determines the odds for a game or electoral forecasters predict an election. The computers use statistical techniques that have been used for decades usually targeting risk. More data and more computing power have supercharged these techniques. The predict the likelihood of you opening an email, or opening an ad, or default on a loan. They predict you getting sick or being in a car wreck. Predictive analytics are used to make decisions. The challenge is that these algorithms are black boxes. Proponents say the human brain is a black box too.

If a judge decides to put you away for twenty years, that decision is a black box as well. But algorithms are on auto pilot. Actually, automatic pilot is another algorithm. Airlines rely on it because it is more reliable than human pilots. The same is happening in many other sectors. But should a computer be making decisions about a human life? Without meeting the human, examining the emotions or seeing the person's expressions? (Metz, 2020).

Then there is the question of AI and faith. Can our present religious systems survive with AI? Many AI and faith groups focus on whether global religions will remain culturally relevant, and that those texts and traditions of the last many centuries are not discarded and made irrelevant. Humans have always had ineffable qualities that set them apart from everything else. If Alexa offers spiritual advice should you take it seriously? That is getting into people's minds and memories. It gets into how people think about the world. Some of their ethical positions and how they think about and value their own lives. In 1984 Sherry Turkle at MIT wrote a book *The Second Self* where she talks about human and computer relationships. Her stance was that humans would embrace computers for reason, and we would retain our feelings of spirit and soul. Since then, the relationship humans have with machines has grown much more complex. Our spirits and souls are much more mixed up with our data, screens and devices (Kinstler, 2021). This is not only true while we are alive and on this planet.

Is it okay to digitally reincarnate people? The film made to reincarnate Antony Bourdain, *Roadrunner*, created considerable controversy because of its use of AI. It used several hours of conversations taped by Mr. Bourdain while he was still alive to create 45 seconds of his voice in new audio. When you watch the film you don't really know which lines were spoken by AI, and which were not. It sounds just like Bourdain. Because we live in a digital world, we leave a trail of voice, email and text messages along with social media profiles. Digital surveillance is with us all the time. People enter more than 1.8 million Google searches every minute and send more than 188 million emails. Public social media accounts stay up until someone takes them down. Private exchanges, like the one that provided the email read in the Bourdain documentary, present other ethical questions. Would he have wanted his voice recreated by AI? Or his private emails read on camera? Of course, if you are dead, you can't consent, but often families can't or don't recover online data of the deceased. Like so much else with AI it is dualistic. Images and words of those who have passed can be soothing memories or they can be abused. Because of the Pandemic years, many funerals were digital. Are we headed for digital memorial parks where people meet up with deceased loved ones' avatars in VR? If so who will regulate that (Matei, 2021)?

There is also the case for accountability. The AI Incident Database launched in late 2020 is an attempt at tracking AI "no nos." Some examples are a security robot that ended up in a fountain and Google Photo tracking black people as gorillas. It is hosted by a nonprofit. It is founded by the large tech companies. The purpose is to research what happens when technology goes wrong. The rationale was that the culture of software engineering doesn't encourage safety. At the same time, AI is finding the way more directly into people's lives. The database uses a broad definition of AI. It contains everything from YouTube

Kids displaying adult content to glitches in the French welfare system. Anyone can submit a calamity to the database. One of the most humorous is a facial recognition system in China that incorrectly accused a woman of jaywalking. It was from a picture on the side of a bus (Simonite, 2021).

Fears about how AI might transform our lives have been around for decades. In the 1940s Isaac Asimov asserted a robot may not injure or harm a human being through action or inaction. Science fiction pitted robots and humans against each other like HAL 9000 in the 1968 film *2001: A Space Odyssey*. But what these futurists did not address is the impact of AI's broad and potentially more significant effect on human interactions. Social norms and ethics along with morals and reactions have developed in homo sapiens over thousands of years. Regardless of where you are in the world, love, friendship, cooperation and teaching remain remarkably consistent. It doesn't matter whether they use technologies or not or if they are urban or rural. Adding AI to the mix could very easily disrupt these social structures.

Robots created to show empathy and admit mistakes are more compatible with the human condition. Hybrid systems where humans and robots interact socially can improve connections between humans. Bots used in other ways have shown that they can turn generous people into very selfish jerks. We saw in 2016 how AI can corrupt outside the laboratory. Trolling and malevolent Russian accounts attacked Twitter in the run up to the U.S. presidential election. Many of these were bots. They influenced conservative users particularly strongly. They polarized the country's electorate. Digital assistants are becoming pervasive. Many people treat them as friends and confidants. The effects on children and growing up without empathic connections remains unknown. AI continues to expand into our lives. it is important to examine the possibilities of stunting our emotions. AI could inhibit empathy leaving human to human relationships more shallow and more selfish.

Is the Cat out of The Bag with AI?

AI could affect humans in ways we haven't yet anticipated. Let's use driving as an example. Driving is a modern kind of social interaction. It requires cooperation and social coordination. Some self-driving cars are also designed to take over from humans before accidents happen. They predict and take over with the power to make moral judgments. The real issue is to look before we leap. Let's consider the impact of AI on the bigger picture and society as a whole. Asimov said in 1985, "Injury to a person can be analyzed and judged, Humanity is an abstraction." Assessing the harm of these new technologies to humanity over time must surely be a part of the equation.

There are so many big questions and so far, not many answers. Because the effects on humans can be intense and far reaching, it's time to discuss what broader impacts might emerge, where human intervention is needed and how regulation might benefit the common good. There are tough questions to ask like: Should we trust personal devices like Alexa? The IOT? What about our children's safety? Privacy? Development? The part of this revolution that needs to come front and center is the part that impacts core aspects of life for humans. It is imperative to take steps to assure that AI can live constructively with us. We need to put into place regulations that enhance compatibility between the growth of new technologies and AI's ability to live with human beings (Christakis, 2019).

Microsoft was one of the earliest companies to take a position on ethics. In 2016, CEO Satya Nadella spoke at a conference. He highlighted that Microsoft was positioned for the use of AI to support and augment human capabilities. Microsoft was building trust into AI products. The next year they formed a cross-functional committee to investigate ethics and AI in research and engineering. In 2018 Deloitte interviewed AI executives and found that 32% ranked ethics in the top three concerns. Microsoft created a role focused on AI ethics, advocacy and evangelism. They hired a man named Tim O'Brien. He had a history with the company as a General Manager for over 15 years. This is certainly a role many organizations might consider. The issues surrounding AI ethics are complex. They need to be discussed and examined by many great minds.

O'Brien began his work as an AI Ethicist by traveling around the globe. He gave talks and presented at conferences. He spoke about topics like avoiding bias in AI algorithms and creating transparency in AI modules. He focused on AI but promoted ethical perspectives in all aspects of information technologies. Many applications of technology in the real world have been void of ethical examination. This includes analytics, IOT, virtual and augmented reality and of course AI. O'Brien's goal is to develop a global perspective on it and to include cultural awareness. Some societies around the world have very different perspectives on privacy and ethics. China will tolerate facial recognition and social credit scores. Germany is more privacy oriented, perhaps because of the infiltration of East German spies.

England doesn't mind cameras on a main street in London but that might reflect IRA bombings in the past. O'Brien's work includes the analysis of cultures and the integration of many sources of information and research (Davenport, 2019).

The challenge as we move forward is not just new policies within Microsoft but a global initiative. There are many questions within Microsoft yet to be asked and there are more on the global stage. What are the legal ramifications of harm from AI? Companies that create this type of ethics role need to have strong backing from leadership and senior executives. Business and organizations that use AI and other technologies are facing these questions or will face them in the future. Having an internal position or committee focused on examining this as it unfolds might be useful.

ASK THE HARD QUESTIONS

- What can be done to hold companies accountable for privacy and ethics in AI?
- What do humans lose when we let AI make decisions?
- What new policies do we need for regulation of AI?
- Should certain topics be off limits with AI?
- Can we get control of privacy and ethics? Is it too Late?

Chapter 14

Working With Humans

> "Despite all the hype and excitement about AI, it's still extremely limited today relative to what human intelligence is."
> —Andrew Ng

There is no question AI will continue to evolve. It promises to have the largest impact on human living of any technology to date. It will change the way we look at knowledge and mechanical automation and the way we view proper principles of reasoning. Over the last few decades AI has achieved great things. It has been able to help solve intellectual problems both theoretical and real. We planned and built robots that -controlled human touch, sight and self-awareness. AI has helped to translate languages, chart routes and provide instruction to learn new skills and gain new knowledge. Some efforts have been highly successful and some fundamental. Either way it has focused on what it is to be human and have human capabilities. Although AI is often used to describe a list of methods or a catch-all label, what it actually entails is the enduring and intriguing goals of understanding intelligent beings and instructing intelligent systems.

Discussions of AI tend to focus on the failures rather than the successes. AI has its foundations in mathematical modeling and cognitive behavior modeling. It creates autonomous agents or robots. It combines multiple agents to identify knowledge, representation and procedures. These are needed for the agents to work together or around each other. It develops algorithms for analysis of speech, language, videos, images, diagrams and photographs. It represents knowledge and articulates it. AI allows us to reflect, plan and act. It helps in making decisions, constructing plans and designing pathways. Through knowledge, representation and articulation it is capable of learning and adaption. It has already caused major shifts in many fields. Some examples are linguistics, psychology, philosophy and organizational theory.

The practical application of AI expands every day. Neutral networks have automated everything. AI is found everywhere from breast cancer diagnoses to online handwriting recognition. Bots have replaced help desks and customer service systems. Speech recognition technology has had a huge commercial impact. In the future these and many other areas will continue to expand. Look for AI to act more naturally with people. It will develop a degree of self-understanding and integrity. Successful AI endeavors will learn as they evolve. They will continue to adapt to changes in the environment.

Amazon's Alexa is a good example of a system that adapts to changes in the environment. It engages in extended dialogue. It increasingly tries to clarify and enrich its depth of understanding. AI is successful in narrow fields. It will probably stay that way for a while. AI can model rationale in customer experiences and decision theory supporting collaboration. It can enhance communications and obtain knowledge. It can generate intelligent action and deepen the mathematical models that are AI's foundation. AI reasoning systems are showing up in traditional programs. This makes it easier to mix computation and reasoning to achieve a desired result.

Robots working in data-rich environments require little investment. The existing systems and networks provide their foundations. Longer term goals for AI will combine vision, touch, speech and other senses into everyday tasks. Rational thinking forms the foundation of cognitive modeling. Economic judgment promises to play an even greater role in the development of AI. AI will use logic to help us solve problems and meet goals. AI theories relating goals and preferences provides one step in this direction.

Expect collaborative systems to blossom. This draws together many areas of AI research including planning, learning, speech and language. It involves the fundaments of communication and methods of resolving conflict. It provides a good environment for tackling problems. People will work together with AI agents in a common environment. They will share models. This will allow each entity to convey knowledge and share discoveries. Collaboration is the foundation for expansion. AI and humans working together.

Trust will not be easy. Uncertainty, intent and thinking while speaking are big obstacles. What people say or write and what they actually mean can be different. NLP (Natural Language Processing) and effective user interfaces are opportunities as AI evolves. Traditional computer systems focus on automating processes. Intelligent systems support explanation, guidance, maintenance and learning. We can look forward to AI automating more routine and data intensive areas. This includes commercial, industrial and scientific research. Computer systems will be more natural. They will be easier to use and more capable of acting as independent AI workers (Doyle & Dean, 1997).

People chronically overestimate what AI can do now. They underestimate what it can do in the next decade. Depending on where you start, the AI revolution began over a half century ago. A combination of greater computing speeds and larger and larger amounts of data formed the foundation for AI. Where we are now, it is easy to recognize many of the mistakes. We waited too long to realize the implications of and damage done by important choices in technology. We left those choices up to private interests and profits. From automobiles creating the suburbs to Facebook and misinformation, mistakes in managing this technology are apparent everywhere (Fallows, 2021).

AI Amnesia At the center of the study of cognitive systems is the idea of problem-solving. Classical cognitive science uses two distinct approaches. It provides a conceptual framework for examining intelligence. Cognitive psychology focuses only on humans. Cognitive science is IDC (Individual Distributed Cognition) and SDC (System Distributed Cognition). It explores how information is represented in the cognitive system. It examines how this information is spread to achieve goal-oriented behaviors. The aim is to understand intelligence. And to understand how it is displayed at the system level not just the individual level. The study of distributed cognition focuses on calculations needed to perform work (European Conference of Cognitive Science, 1999).

Companies use machine learning to analyze people's expressions, likes and dislikes, faces and emotions. If machines can learn, they can be trained to unlearn. This unlearning could give people ownership and control over their own data. Some companies will allow people to delete their personal data. People generally don't understand algorithms. They are in the dark. They don't know how their data is being used. They are not compensated for it. Unlearning could make it possible for companies to stop exploiting people or to compensate them.

The FTC (Federal Trade Commission) is taking a closer look at the power of algorithms. Regulation of personal data will provide the hope that individuals will have a little more say so over the use of their data. The attitude toward blind technology advancement is changing. The privacy risks are real. Awareness and concern about these are growing in the U.S. and Europe. Apple, Microsoft and Google all use something called differential privacy. This puts constraints on what a system can leak about an individual. The problem is it is rarely used. There is no doubt that individual privacy risks are plentiful.

AI's Social Conscience

There is no question that social responsibility will be part of technology in the future. What is called technology engineering will change. Now it is just trying to accurately predict cancer diagnoses or supply chain movements. Soon it will include how people interpret these predictions and whether they have the potential for harm. Building AI has become simple. Figuring out its effect on people is much harder. A program called Delphi is still in the development stage. It tries to teach AI about human values. Some people diametrically oppose Delphi or any other attempt to teach AI values. They say this type of research furthers the false notion that AI can or should be given the responsibility to make ethical judgments. The jury is still out.

There are many examples of AI gone wrong. Microsoft released a chatbot in 2016 named Tay designed to learn online conversation and it quickly learned hateful, biased and offensive things. It was taken off the market. Some systems have developed output algorithms that are being trained to filter and monitor hateful language and bias. Many believe that these specific examples are only the tip of the iceberg and inform us of broader and wider problems in AI (Simonite, 2021).

Only the Rich Can Play

The costs of training AI are rising. Microsoft builds one 4 times bigger than the biggest model. China builds one bigger. The idea that larger models can unlock new capabilities is dominating the tech industry. Ten years ago, a PhD student working hard could explore work that was state of the art. Not today. This cuts down on innovation and puts the power with the biggest companies. Those that can afford to play. At the same time, science is pushing people to get more efficient and effective in developing AI. Tesla is developing its own chips for AI autonomous driving. Dozens of other companies are working on chips for training and running AI. People are working on ways to specialize machine learning, training and making neural networks smaller and more affordable. It's a question of three variables: accuracy, speed and cost. People with considerable influence are interested in making AI open source. This would democratize AI for companies without AI expertise. This comes with its own risks. It will certainly promote adoption, but what else is at stake?

For now, the AI industry is highly concentrated in the San Francisco Bay Area. This is a concern. As these localized companies compete against each other for resources and talent, it locks in a winner-take-most mentality. There is hope that the federal government will get in the game. Hopes that they can start to fund startups in diverse locations. The Feds might invest in new and different AI clusters to provide balance. This is what happened during the micro revolution when Boston competed against North Carolina which competed against the West Coast.

The impact on people's everyday lives is expected to grow. Government and business continue to adopt the technologies in many forms and for many reasons. AI can increase productivity. There is also a concern that it will give more wealth and power to the people who already have wealth and power. Cities that can support the talent pipelines needed to feed AI will reap the benefits.

There is also a downside. It's not yet known how many will get left behind. Currently six out of ten computer science and engineering college degrees are awarded to foreign-born students. As AI continues to grow, job loss from automation is inevitable. To attract and retain AI talent, regions will need to invest in better high schools and community colleges. They will need to increase tax breaks and expand other educational opportunities. Higher Education needs to include a focus on topics like machine learning, high performance computing, semiconductors and advancing computer hardware. (Johnson, 2021).

AI Invades HR

The adoption of AI in HR is growing fast. The real question is "Is HR Implementing AI Intelligently?" Trying to cope with the COVID pandemic shifted the emphasis to the remote workplace. This enabled digitalization. It created conditions for digital dexterity irrespective of industries. Companies quickly changed their plans. They re-prioritized their technology so they could cope with remote and hybrid workers. Digital competencies are now a requirement across all levels in nearly all organizations. HR still has a long way to go. What is still needed is a mindset shift from reaction to responding. There is no doubt that workforce dynamics has a direct impact on business performance.

HR is starting to use data analytics and identify data sets that might be useful. There is a big difference between data that is easy to get and data that is actually useful. AI can help HR infer job skills, propensity to learn and retention rates. What AI can't do yet is confidently predict the best next action for a desired outcome. Humans are just too complex. It's not that the technology doesn't exist. It is just that those humans are still building AI systems with algorithms that are unintentionally biased, unpredictable or vulnerable to misinformation.

For AI to be effective it needs to make sure that the data has integrity. It needs to be built into the HRIS, LMS or LXPs, talent acquisition platforms. Most AI integration is provided by third party vendors. This has limitations. The challenge comes in getting HR departments ready to share insights. They will need data literacy and to understand predictive skills. Hierarchical organizational charts may become a thing of the past. AI can help HR build a pool of talent that has the expertise, experience and skills necessary to transform the way we work (HR Exchange Network Editorial Team, 2021).

Content Intelligence and Skills Development

Online content development is on the rise. It has been growing for decades. Large organizations often spend millions on content libraries. Often they have little idea of what is relevant to employees. A large communication firm in Philadelphia had a library of thirty-two courses on climbing a telephone pole. Apparently there are only three ways to do it. This unfortunately is typical of large L&D departments.

The bricks vs clicks debate has gone on for a long time, but technology has continued to evolve.

Intelligent content is on the move. It has many forms, mobile, micro, macro, synchronous, asynchronous, off the shelf, customized, compliance or employee authored. The market for eLearning content has exploded. Worth in excess of 300 billion dollars, the market for digital learning is enormous. Learners are inundated with choices, maybe too many choices.

Online learning platforms and vendors are cashing in. L&D departments have no way of really knowing which content is relevant and aligned with their needs.

The term LRS or Learning Record Store has been around for a while. Rather than searching for data in an LMS (Learning Management System) or a LXP (Learning Experience Platform), the LRS can be a single source that keeps the learning data in one place. The missing link was intelligence. The LRS generates information on skill development after the investment in content is made. Adding AI to the mix allows for better forecasting. It can replace quantity with quality and invest in more high value content. Most skills training in organizations is a shot in the dark. Courses are analyzed by consumption numbers or judged by the title of the course. Often very little is known about assessments and application let alone alignment to the individual's or company needs. This is where AI can be useful. AI can combine vast amounts of data and look for alignment to relevance, engagement and applicability. It can position the LRS in context unique to each organization's needs (Nangia, 2022).

Smarter Demand Forecasting

IKEA is using AI to forecast demand for its products. This is an example of using AI well. The AI they use is called "Demand Planning." It helps them forecast year-round sales demand for 450 IKEA stores across 54 markets. It draws the data from over 200 sources. It can estimate demand for stores that can fluctuate by day of the week or time of the year. In total the sum of all of these products could be in the billions. Supply chain fluctuations are an important number to IKEA. As a retailer, they stock shelves and that costs money. Having too many or too few products for customers can result from shopping preferences fluctuation because of weather forecasts or seasonal changes or local festivals.

Demand Planning operates at 98% efficiency. It builds knowledge from a local perspective with the customer at the center. It goes from forecasting at a local level to a market, country, region and global demand and supply. It works smartly and across online and face to face channels. It is agile and can adapt to new store layouts, selling capabilities and customer behaviors. The fact that it is agile and allows for manual overrides helps to ensure better availability of products and better customer relations. It cuts down on costs. These savings can be passed on to the consumer. Predictive planning with the use of AI is a big area and one that will continue to grow (IKEA, 2021).

AI Attorneys The legal profession used to have large libraries full of books. Lawyers spent late nights poring over written cases trying to extract information that helped clients. Not anymore. AI is being leveraged across a large range of applications. Budgets for technologies in law are increasing by over 50% annually. The legal industry is using AI for legal research, self-service online, litigation strategies, dispute resolution and contract review. AI has helped to improve research outcomes. It frees up humans to engage with clients. AI allows much more comprehensive predictions. It can quickly examine larger data sets far beyond any one lawyer's human experiences. Machine learning can review volumes of contracts for due diligence or identify certain clauses and outliers. AI is firmly entrenched in the legal services industry and there is no turning back (Thomson Reuters, 2020).

Healthcare for Humans

Should doctors be replaced by AI? That depends. There are certain fields in medicine that might be better done with AI. This has already been demonstrated with narrow AI in areas like skin cancer research. Still other areas are much better left in the hands of human doctors or perhaps doctors and AI working together, and each doing what it does best. AI can identify patterns, read vast amounts of data to predict outcomes, use information to recommend nutritional advice and create medical records while doctors are seeing the patients using voice commands, allowing doctors to focus on human interactions. Humans are able to put a diagnosis in context, recommend tests and scans, offer emotional support and interact with family members. Again, the emphasis is on humans and machines working together not one replacing the other (Topol, 2019).

Playing Catch Up

AI should be used in Higher Education to open channels of participation. It can help bridge the access to quality learning. Technology can help sidestep the constraints of time and location. It can ensure lifelong learning opportunities for everyone. AI has the capabilities of promoting collaboration across boundaries, curiosity and creativity. Many academics hope that AI will do for Higher Education what it already does in industry. AI streamlines workflows and processes. Virtual assistants like Jill

Watson at the Georgia Institute of Technology have been answering FAQ for students since 2016. Jill answers repeatedly asked questions for a graduate class in AI. The adoption of AI in Higher Ed is still very low even though it offers a great deal of promise. Many institutions are skeptical about implementing AI. Part of the reason is culture. Part of it is cost. Only 41% of universities and colleges have any plans for implementing AI. Only 43% have any AI implementation in the budget (Bouchrika, 2020).

The first AI programs were written in 1950. After a 70-year delay, AI is playing out quickly on so many fronts, it is challenging to keep up. Legal and moral codes is one of them. How do you punish theft in a digital world? Virtual theft is hard to explain. How can you steal something that doesn't exist? Different philosophers have different opinions on both sides of the aisle. How about murder in a virtual world? How is that punished? Banishing the avatar is one way but is that appropriate? AI can comb virtual worlds and let us know what is going on in the metaverse but what about the ethics involved? Those decisions are issues humans need to discuss and soon (Chalmers, 2022).

The impact of the industrial revolution and the digital revolution changed our society. The AI revolution will be similar but more substantial. It will have far reaching effects. The impact on business and employment will be considerable. Global competition will intensify. People are now able to buy goods and services from anywhere in the world. This will intensify as big data is exploited. AI will open unlimited benefits as it becomes more widely used. Competitive advantages will open up for entrepreneurs willing to innovate and turn AI ideas into global success stories. The benefits of AI are worldwide markets with new products and services and immense improvements in productivity. The challenges with AI come with increased unemployment and wealth in the hands of a few. Technologies are taking us from a work environment to a true process/collaboration environment. AI provides constant feedback, learning from the past (workers, clients, processes). AI will help us improve those processes and increase our understanding of how it all comes together.

AI will create an environment where processes are constantly being monitored and analyzed. This will support improvement. AI supports efficiencies to ensure high quality and productivity. Much like the invention of the light bulb or the Internet, AI will find its way into almost everything in our lives. AI will be in banking, personal finance, retail, education, communication, gaming, media, hospitality, entertainment, food, sports, aerospace, healthcare, HR, agriculture, law, real estate, social networks, government, defense, smart homes, smart cities, cyber security, insurance and on and on.

AI will improve transaction-oriented processes, inquiry and information processing. The opportunities are endless. They include the time it takes to process a task and the feedback loop and assessment of synergy between tasks. AI can eliminate tasks with no value (approvals, checks etc.), analyze competition and set benchmarks. It can optimize by assessing skills and knowledge and biofeedback loops and then take steps to improve the processes. AI will include an analysis of success, deeper analysis of outcomes, comparative analysis and time driven analysis. AI will be responsive to the business need and the convergence of need with new technologies. This will lead to great and greater adaption.

Digital transformations accelerated with the COVID pandemic that started in 2020. The world changed, and the world of work was changed forever. Nine to five is dead. What will replace it? The four-day work week? Maybe. But experts say there is a shift from an emphasis on time to skills. AI can Identify the skills the workforce needs, make an inventory and determine which ones are available. As technology plays a larger part in skilling and upskilling the workforce, there is a shift toward humanizing work. This realignment involves putting the worker at the center. Companies must invest in learning and bring a human element into data and AI. The more technology we use, the more important it is to bring the human back into focus. It's important to build relationships and friendships that last and create deep links and collaborative environments.

AI is not one thing, and a lot of things call themselves AI. It's important to remember the gold is in the data. AI algorithms are only as good as the data sets they are using. AI is here to help humans solve problems and automate processes. It is not something that exists in isolation. AI is AI until you understand what it is doing and then it is just software. It's only ever as good as the data. Understanding the data, where it is and what shape it is in, is critical to considering how AI might apply to your organization. AI is not a replacement for humans but can serve humans by enhancing the human experience. AI is changing and will continue to change the way we do almost everything.

AI is all around us but much of it is invisible. It seems mysterious and futuristic, but it is here, and it is changing our lives. Everywhere you turn there is a bot, a personal assistant or an advisor making suggestions and recommending alternatives. Machines generate a lot of the newsfeeds you receive. AI is responsible for the information you come in contact with. This includes news about sports, finance, politics and global concerns. Companies will continue to invest in new tools. It is important to keep looking forward, but it is also critical to put human needs first. There is no way to go back. This has been proven time and time again. There is no reset button or reversal switch. Technology never goes back. Technology brings change and change brings new opportunities.

References

Al-Hudhud G. (2012) Intelligent System Design Requirements for Personalized e-Learning Systems: Applications of AI to Education. King Saud University, Riyadh. KSA.

Ali, A. (2020) The Soaring Value of Intangible Assets in S&P 500. Retrieved July 16, 2021 from https://www.visualcapitalist.com/the-soaring-value-of-intangible-assets-in-the-sp-500/

Allen, C. (2016) The Path to Self-Sovereign identity. Retrieved April 4, 2021 from http://lifewithalacrity.com/2016/the-path-to-self-soverereign-idenity.html

Ames, P. (2019) Are we automating ourselves into obsolescence? Retrieved on February 24, 2020 from https://workflowotg.com/are-we-automating-ourselves-into-obsolescence/

Andriessen, J. and Sanburg, J. (1999). Where is education heading and how about AI? International Journal of Artificial Intelligence in Education, 10, 130-150.

AVIDCHANGE (2018) Will Accountants Become Obsolete? Retrieved April 20, 2019 from http://www.advidxchange.com/will-accountants-become-obsolete

Baggio, B. (2017) The Rebirth of Higher Education. Presented to Drexel University, eLearning 3.0 Conference, March 30, 2017.

Baggio, B. (2020) AI and Education Reborn. March 29, 2020. International Conference on Complexity, Informatics and Cybernetics: IMCIC 2020

Baggio, B. & Omana, N. (2019) AI and Big Workplace Changes. Workforce Solutions Review. April-June 2019. ihrim.org

Baggio, B. and Omana, N. (2019) AI and the Agile Workplace. 10th International Multi-Conference on Complexity, Informatics and Cybernetics: IMCIC 2019, Orlando, FL.

Berman, B. (2021) Latest data show that intangible assets comprise 90% of the valuation of the S&P 500 Companies. Retrieved July 12, 2021 from https://ipcloseup.com/2021/01/19/latest-data-show-that-intangible-assets-comprise-90-of-the-value-of-the-sp-500-companies/

BMJ (2018) Could Machines Using Artificial Intelligence Make Doctors Obsolete? Retrieved April 20, 2019 from http://sciencedaily.com/releases/2018

Bouchrika, I. (2020) Embracing Artificial Intelligence for Learning. Retrieved on March 13, 2022, from https://research.com/education/trends-in-higher-education#ai

Brander, S. Hinkelmann, K., Martin, A. and Thonssen, B. (2011). Mining of Agile Business Processes. AAAI 2011 Spring Symposium. p. 9-14.

Brooker, K. (2019). Google on the brain. Fast Company. October 2019. p.76-92.

Broome, K. (2018). Who Invented Education? Retrieved from https://sciencetrends.com/invented-school-created-standardized-education/ on December 09, 2019.

Brougham, D. and Haar, J. (2017). Smart Technology, Artificial Intelligence, Robotics, and Algorithms (STARA): Employees' perceptions of our future workplace. January 2017Journal of Management & Organization 24(2):1-19.

Brown, A. (2019) 11 Quotes About AI That'll Make You Think .Retrieved September 6, 2019 from https://www.techopedia.com/11-quotes-about-ai-thatll-make-you-think/2/33718

Bryar, C. & Carr, B. (2021) Have we taken agile too far? Harvard Business Review. April 09, 2021. Retrieved June 18, 2021 from https://hbr.org/2021/04/have-we-taken-agile-too-far

Buchanan, B. (2006). A (Very) Brief History of Artificial Intelligence. AI Magazine, December 2005.

Bughin, J. & Manyka, J. (2021) Measuring the full impact of digital capital.

Carr, A., Dat, M., Frier S., Gurman M. (2019) Yes They are listening: How Silicon Valleys' Biggest Companies Got Millions of People to Let Temps Analyze Their Conversations. Bloomsberg Business Week. December 16, 2019.

Casey, K. (2021). 5 Robotic Process Automation (RPA) trends to watch in 2021. The Enterprisers Project.

Castellina, N. (2018) How Artificial Intelligence is Transforming the Manufacturing Workforce. Retrieved on May 9, 2018 from http://www.mbtmag.com/home/article13246376

Cellan-Jones, R. (2014, December 2) Stephan Hawking warns artificial intelligence could end mankind. *BBC News*.

Chalmers, D. (2022) What Should Be Considered a Crime in the Metaverse? Retrieved on March 13, 2022 from https://www.wired.com/story/crime-metaverse-virtual-reality/

Christakis, N. (2019) How AI Will Rewire Us. Atlantic. April 2019. Retrieved 3/3/2022 from https://www.theatlantic.com/magazine/archive/2019/04/robots-human-relationships/583204/?CNDID=4976163&mbid=nl_031319_daily_list1_p5&source=DAILY_NEWSLETTER

Chui, M., Manyika, J. and Miremadi, M. (2105). Four fundamentals of workplace automation. McKinsey Quarterly, November 2015.

Cognizant (2017). 21 Jobs of the Future: A guide to Getting and Staying Employed Over the Next 10 Years Retrieved on May 10, 2021 from https://www.cognizant.com/whitepapers/21-jobs-of-the-future-a-guide-to-getting-and-staying-employed-over-the-next-10-years-codex3049.pdf

Cognizant (2018). 21 More Jobs of the Future: A Guide to Getting and Staying Employed Through 2029. Retrieved May 10, 2021 from https://www.cognizant.com/whitepapers/21-more-jobs-of-the-future-a-guide-to-getting-and-staying-employed-through-2029-codex3928.pdf

Cohen, J. (2017) Does the Rise of AI precede the end of code? Retrieved on May 5, 2021 from http://www.itproportal.com/features/does-the-rise-of-ai-preced-the-end-of-code

Cohn, C. (2021) The Right to Digital Privacy. The New York Times, Sunday August 8, 2021. 7.

Computer History Museum, (2019). Data General Corporation. Retrieved on October 1, 2019 from https://www.computerhistory.org/brochures/d-f/

Cornerstone. (2018) 3 Crucial ways to mee the onboarding needs of the modern workforce. Retrieved February 18, 2020 from https://www.cornerstoneondemand.com/resources/briefs/3-crucial-way-meet-onboarding-needs-modern-workforce

Corsi-Bunker, A. (2006). Guide to the Educational System of the United States, ISSS, (International Student Services), University of Minnesota. https://isss.umn.edu/publications/USEducation/2.pdf

COSN (2019) Driving K-12 education, hurdles and accelerators. Retrieved December, 19, 2019 from https://cosn.org/k12innovation/hurdles-accelerators.

Crawford, K. (2016, June 25) Artificial Intelligence's White Guy Problem. New York Times, p. 1-4

Davenport, T. (2019) The AI Advantage; How to Put the Artificial Intelligence Revolution to Work. The MIT Press, Cambridge, MA, London, UK. p.24-59

Davenport, T. (2019) What Does an AI Ethicist Do? Retrieved February 24, 2022 from http://sloanreview.mit.edu/article/what-does-an-ai-ethist-do/

Deloitte (2019) Introducing HR's new, not so human, resource. ConnectMe.

Deloitte (2019) Leading the social enterprise: Reinvent with human focus. 2019 Deloitte Global Human Capital Trends. Retrieved on May 7, 2020 from https://www2.deloitte.com/content/dam/insights/us/articles/5136_HC-Trends-2019/DI_HC-Trends-2019.pdf

Deloitte (2019) State of AI in the Enterprise, 2nd Ed. https://www2.deloitte.com/content/dam/insights/us/articles/4780_State-of-AI-in-the-enterprise/DI_State-of-AI-in-the-enterprise-2nd-ed.pdf

Deming, D. (2020) Robots Are Coming We Need to Get Smart. New York Times February 2. 2020.

Dilmegani, C. (2021) What is RPA? In depth definition and guide to RPA 2021 Retrieved July 12, 2021, from http://reseach.aimultiple.com/what-is-robotic-process-automation/

Doyle, J. and Dean T. (1997) Strategic Directions in Artificial Intelligence. AI Magazine Volume 18. P. 87-101.

Duren, T. (2019) 9 Artificial Intelligence Trends You Should Keep an Eye On In 2019. Retrieved September 6, 2019 from https://hackernoon.com/future-artificial-intelligence-2019-1cd09cc491c7

European Conference on Cognitive Science (1999) IDC and SDC A Common Heritage. Siena Italy, p.87-92

Fallows, J. (2021) The Real Machine Age. New York Times Sunday April 4, 2021. Book Review. p10.

Farrow, K. (2019. AI Predictions for 2019: Artificial Intelligence Boldly Goes Where No One Has Gone Before. Retrieved on March 23, 2022 from https://blogs.oracle.com/oracleuniversity/post/ai-predictions-for-2019-artificial-intelligence-boldly-goes-where-no-one-has-gone-before?intcmp=WWOUBLOGPOSTOPKFAI110619

Goldstein, P. (2017) What Happened to Wang Computers: How the Wang 2200 Reinvented Office IT. Retrieved October 1, 2019 from https://biztechmagazine.com/article/2017/04/advent-office-pcs-wang-2200-reigned-computing-dynamo

Gons, E., Ketzener, L., Carson, B., Peddicord, T., & Mallory, G., (2018. How AI and Robotics Will Disrupt the Defense Industry. Bosaton Consulting Group.

Goodwin, D. (2016) Digital Equipment Corporation (DEC): a Case Study of Indecision, Innovation and Company Failure. Retrieved August 26 from https://dare.uva.nl/search?identifier=6bd9edc0-f2c0-4bc7-9523-3178a5d2ac57

Growth Stage Podcast. (2018, August 1). Robots Are Our Friends. Boston, MA, US.

Gruver, G. & Mouser, T. (2015) *Leading Transformation: Applying Agile Principles at Scale*. IT Revolution, Portland OR. ISBN: 978-1-942788-01-0

He, E. (2108) The year when AI will humanize the workplace. Retrieved on September 7, 2019 from https://blogs.oracle.com/oraclehcm/2018-the-year-when-ai-will-humanize-the-workplace

Heller, M. (2021) How to choose RPA software:10 factors to consider. Retrieved June 17, 2021 from https://www.cio.com/article/3621728/how-to-choose-rpa-software-for-your-business.html

Hill, K. (2021) Your Face is Not Your Own. The New York Times Magazine. Sunday, March 21, 2021. 32-49.

Hirsch, V. (2017, February 19). AI and the Future of Work. Work and Life in the Age of Robots. TEDx. Manchester, UK.

Holley, P. (2019) Giant Stores will place robotic assistants in 172 locations, company says. Retrieved January 10, 2020 from http://www.wasahingtonpost.com/technology/2019/01/04/giant-food-stores-will-place-robotic-assistants-inside-locations-compnay-says?

Househ, S. (2018) Examining the value of a college degree. Retrieved on September 3, 2019 from https://www.chieflearningofficer.com/2018/12/18/examining-the-value-of-a-college-degree/

HR Examiner, 2021. The Heart of AI Utility in HRTech. Retrieved August 11, 2021 from http://hrexaminer.com/mainentance-is-the-heart-of-ai-utility-in-hr-tech

HR Exchange Network Editorial Team (2021). AI In the Future of HR with Wagner Denuzzo. Retrieved March 12, 2022 from https://www.hrexchangenetwork.com/hr-tech/interviews/qa-ai-in-the-future-of-hr-with-wagner-denuzzo

Hyatt, J. (2003) The Business That Time Forgot Data General is gone. But does that make its founder a failure? Retrieved October 1, 2019 from https://money.cnn.com/magazines/fsb/fsb_archive/2003/04/01/341000/

IBA Global Employment Institute, Artificial Intelligence and Robotics and Their Impact on the Workplace. April 21017.

IBM (2021) What is robotic process automation? Retrieved June 29, 2021 from https://www.ibm.com/cloud/learn/rpa.

IKEA (2021) Using artificial intelligence for smarter demand forecasting. Retrieved on March 13, 2022 from https://about.ikea.com/en/life-at-home/behind-the-scenes/2021/05/27/using-artificial-intelligence-for-smarter-demand-forecasting

Jenkins, R. (2019). Here are eight seismic shifts that will impact how employees learn and develop in the future. Retrieved on December 10, 2019 from https://www.inc.com/ryan-jenkins/8-big-shifts-in-learning-development-you-need-to-know.html.

Johal, S. (2017) Technology Will Make Today's Government Obsolete and That's Good. Retrieved on April 5, 2019 from the http://www.conversation.com/technology-will-make-todays-government-obsolete-and-that's-good-86430

Johnson, K. (2021) In the US, the AI Industry Risks Becoming Winner-Take-Most. Retrieved March 12, 2022 from https://www.wired.com/story/us-ai-industry-risks-becoming-winner-take-most/?bxid=5cec28123f92a45b30f3bf54&cndid=4976163&esrc=Wired_etl_load&source=EDT_WIR_NEWSLETTER_0_TRANSPORTATION_ZZ&utm_brand=wired&utm_campaign=aud-dev&utm_content=A&utm_mailing=WIR_Daily_091321_FastForward&utm_medium=email&utm_source=nl&utm_term=WIR_TopClickers_EXCLUDE_Transportation

Kahn, A. (2019) 9 Artificial Intelligence Trends You Should Keep An Eye On In 2019

Retrieved on March 31, 2019 from https://hackernoon.com/future-artificial-intelligence-2019-1cd09cc491c7

Kanungo, S. (2018). Disruptive Innovation. Keynote Speaker-Disruptive Innovation Conference.

Kinstler, (2021) Can Silicon Valley Find God? Sunday July 18, 2021 The New York Times.

Knight, W. (2018) *Nine charts that really bring home just how fast AI is growing.* MIT Technology Review.

Krasadakis, G. (2018) Artificial Intelligence: the impact on employment and the workforce. Retrieved on May 8, 2021 from https://medium.com/innovation-machine/artificial-intelligence-3c6d80072416

Kwet, M. (2019) Retail Stores Track Your Every Move. The New York Times, Sunday July 16, 2019. 5.

L.A. Times (1992) Troubled Wang Decides to File for Chapter 11: Technology: The once-successful computer firm is $550 million in debt. It failed to keep pace with change. Retrieved from https://www.latimes.com/archives/la-xpm-1992-08-19-fi-5728-story.html

Lawton, G. (2021) What is robotic process automation? Retrieved July 12, 2021 from https://searchcio.techtarget.com/definition/RPA

Lederman, D. (2017) Clayton Christensen doubling down. Retrieved from https://www.insidehighered.com/digital-learning/article/2017/04/28/clay-christensen-sticks-predictions-massive-college-closures on December 08, 2019.

Lee, K. (2018) AI Super-Powers China, Silicon Valley, and the New World Order. Houghton Mifflin Harcourt. Boston and New York. p.204-206.

Lee, K. (2018) What China Can Teach the U.S. about A.I., New York Times, September 23, 2018. SR 5.

Lemoie, K. and Soares, L. (2020) CONNECTED IMPACT Unlocking Education and Workforce Opportunity Through Blockchain. ACE (American Council on Education) Washington, DC.

Leshob, A., Bedard, M., and Mih, H. (2020). Robotic Process Automation and Business Rules: A Perfect Match. ICE-B 2020 7th International Conference on e-Business.

Levitt, T. (2004) Marketing Myopia. July-August Issue. Retrieved October 1, 2019 from https://hbr.org/2004/07/marketing-myopia

Luckin, Rose; Holmes, Wayne; Griÿths, Mark and Forcier, Laurie B. (2016). Intelligence Unleashed: An argument for AI in Education. Pearson Education, London.

Luo, P., Zhoa, Z. Chen, Y. and Ai, W. (2003). Study on multi-agent-based agile supply chain management. International Journal of Advanced Manufacturing Technology 23(3):197-203. February 2004.

Makridakis, S. (2017) The forthcoming artificial intelligence (AI) revolution: Its impact on society and firms. Retrieved September 15, 2019 from http://www.sciencedirect.com/science/article/pii/S0016328717300046

Malone, M. (2000) DEC's Final Demise. Retrieved October 1, 2019 from https://www.forbes.com/2001/01/19/0915malone.html#778e1e561f37

Manning, K. (2020) Intelligent Process Automation vs Robotic Process Automation. Retrieved from https://www.processmaker.com/blog/intelligent-process-automation-ipa-vs-robotic-process-automation-rpa/ on July 12, 2021

Marr, B. (2018) How is AI used in education; Real world examples of today and za peek into the future. Retrieved January 20, 2020 from https://www.forbes.com/sites/bernardmarr/2018/07/25/how-is-ai-used-in-education-real-world-examples-of-today-and-a-peek-into-the-future/#2202e9ac586e

Marshall, A., (2021). AI Comes to Car Repair, and Body Shop Owners Aren't Happy. Retrieved May 10, 2021 from https://www.wired.com/story/ai-car-repair-shop-owners-not-happy/?bxid=5d38d81820122e61c605b7cd&cndid=57963987&esrc=DojoMojoYeti&mbid=mbid%3DCRMWIR012019%0A%0A&source=EDT_WIR_NEWSLETTER_0_DAILY_ZZ&utm_brand=wired&utm_campaign=auddev&utm_mailing=WIR_Daily_041321&utm_medium=email&utm_source=nl&utm_term=list1_p1

Maryville University. (2020) How Blockchain is Used in Education. Retrieved April 5, 2021 from http://online.maryville.edu/blog/blockchain-in-education

Matei, A. (2021). The Contest Over Our Data After We Die. Sunday July 25, 2021. New York Times.

Matthews, K. (2018) 5ways retail robots are disrupting the industry. Retrieved March 1, 202 from http://roboticsbusinessreview.com/retail-hospitality/retail-robots-disrupt-industry .

Matyszczyk, C. (2021) I just watched McDonald's new AI drive thru and I've lost my appetite. Retrieved February 24, 2021, from https://www.zdnet.com/google-amp/article/i-just-watched-mcdonalds-new-ai-drive-thru-and-ive-lost-my-appetite/

McCarthy-Jones, S. Artificial Intelligence is a totalitarian's dream-hers how to take power back.

Retrieved on March 3, 2022 from https://theconversation.com/artificial-intelligence-is-a-totalitarians-dream-heres-how-to-take-power-back-143722

McKinsey & Company (2021). A conversation on artificial intelligence and gender bias. Retrieved March 20, 2022 from https://www.mckinsey.com/featured-insights/asia-pacific/a-conversation-on-artificial-intelligence-and-gender-bias

Melendez, S. (2018) Amazon and Walmart add more jobs but insist they won't terminate jobs. Retrieved on March 1, 2020 from http://www.fastcomapny.com/90279838/amazon-and-walmart-add-more-jobs-but-insist-they-wont-terminate-jobs .

Metz (2020) An Algorithm that Grants Freedom or Takes it Away. New York Times. Sunday, February 9, 2020.

Metz, C. (2021) *Can Artificial Intelligence Be Bias Free?* March 21, 2021. New York Times. NY, NY.

Mircea, M. and Andreescu, A. (2011). Agile Development for Service Oriented Business Intelligence Solutions. *Database Systems Journal. Vol II*, 43-55

Mitchell, A. and Diamond, L. (2018). China's Surveillance State Should Scre Everyoone. The Atlantic.

Moore, A. (2019) When AI becomes an everyday technology. The Daily Alert. Retrieved August 5, 2019 from https://hbr.org/2019/06/when-ai-becomes-an-everyday-technology

Mouser, G. (2015). *Leading the Transformation: Applying Agile and DevOps Principles at Scale.* Portland, OR:IT Revolution.

Narayan, S. (2015) *Agile IT Organization Design. Old Tappan*, NJ: Pearson Education.

Nehal Nangia (2022) The Emergence of Content Intelligence in Learning. Retrieved on March 13, 2022 from https://www.linkedin.com/pulse/emergence-content-intelligence-learning-nehal-nangia/

Nicastro, D. (2021) 8 Examples of Artificial Intelligence in the Workplace. Retrieved on February 24, 2022 from https://www.cmswire.com/digital-workplace/8-examples-of-artificial-intelligence-ai-in-the-workplace/

O'Neil (2017). Why We Need Accountable Algorithms. Retrieved March 15, 2022 from https://www.cato-unbound.org/2017/08/07/cathy-oneil/why-we-need-accountable-algorithms/

Oracle, (2018). The year when AI will humanize the workplace. Retrieved on February 18, 2020 from https://blogs.oracle.com/oraclehcm/2018-the-year-when-ai-will-humanize-the-workplace

Oracle (2019)

Patel, S. (2019). Top 12 Chatbots Trends and Statistics to Follow in 2020. Retrieved from https://www.revechat.com/blog/chatbots-trends-stats/ on December 07, 2019.

Perry, M. (1999) The Application of individually and socially distributed cognition in workplace studies: two peas in a pod? European Conference on Cognitive Science. Siena, Italy. p.87-92.

Pfeiffer, S. (2011) Death Of A Computer Industry Titan: A Conversation With Olsen's Biographer Retrieved on October 1, 2019 from https://www.wbur.org/news/2011/02/08/olsen-biographer

Poeter, D. (2021) Investments in 'intangible assets' like data and branding pay off, McKinsey says. Retrieved on July 16, 2021 from https://www.pye.ai/2021/06/16/investments-in-intangible-assets-like-data-and-branding-pay-off-mckinsey-says/

Porter, E. (2019) Help Wanted: Robots. New York Times. June 16, 2019. SR 11.

Procon.com (2019) Median Incomes v. Average College Tuition Rates. Retrieved from https://college-education.procon.org/median-incomes-v-average-college-tuition-rates/ on December 19, 2019.

PTAC (Privacy Technical Assistance Center) US Department of Education. What is Blockchain? Handout 7, June 2017.

PTAC (Privacy Technical Assistance Center) US Department of Education (2021). The Lifelong Learner: How Blockchain Solutions Can Facilitate Data Transfer and Protect Personal Information for a Lifetime.pdf

Pulist, S.K. (2021) Blockchain Technology Applications in Education. Bulletin of the Technical Committee of Learning Technology. Vol. 21, Number 1, March 16-18 2021.

Quanta Magazine. (2021) A New Approach to Understanding How Machines Think. Retrieved from http://www.Quantamagazine.org/been-kim-is-building a translation for intelligence-20190110 on August, 11, 2021.

Qui, Y. and Xiao, G. (2019) Research on Cost management Optimization of Financial Sharing Center Based on RPA. Procedia ICMIR-2019 3rd International Conference on Mechatronics an Intelligent Robotics.

Rajan, K. (2021) Impact of RPA on business. International Journal of Research in Engineering, Science and Management. Vol. 4., Issue 4., April 2021

Ratliff, E. (2000) O, Engineers! Retrieved on October 1, 2019 from https://www.wired.com/2000/12/soul/

Ratner, P. (2017) AN MIT study predicts when artificial intelligence will take over for humans in different occupations. Retrieved June 4, 2017 from https://bigthink.com/paul-ratner/heres-when-machines-will-take-your-job-predict-ai-gurus

Rimmer, D. (2019) The Power of Digital Assets and Intangibles. Retrieved on July 16, 2021 from https://leadingedgeforum.com/insights/the-power-of-digital-assets-and-intangibles/https://leadingedgeforum.com/insights/the-power-of-digital-assets-and-intangibles/

Robot Ready (2019). Human + Skills for the Future of Work. Strata Institute for the Future of Work, EMSI. Retrieved on August 30, 2019 from https://www.economicmodeling.com/robot-ready-reports/

Rojo, C., Arruda, I., Yuki de Lima Mito, J., Graef, N. Lucizana, A., Ferreira de Scousa, A., & Gomes, S. (2020). *Intangible Assets*. Itaipu Technological Park – PTI Brazil. Osni Hoss.

Ross, M. (2018) 30-years-ago, Digital Equipment Corp., Data General and Wang labs were the biggest companies in Massachusetts. Today they're all gone. What happened to all their vast assets? Retrieved on October 1, 2019 from https://www.quora.com/30-years-ago-Digital-Equipment-Corp-Data-General-and-Wang-labs-were-the-biggest-companies-in-Massachusetts-Today-theyre-all-gone-What-happened-to-all-their-vast-assets

Russel, A. (2006). Apple Computer. Failures of Large Computer Companies.

SAS (2018). Artificial intelligence for executives; Integrating AI into your organization. Retrieved on February 18, 2020 from https://www.sas.com/en_be/whitepapers/artificial-intelligence-for-executives-109066.html

Shethna, J. (2021) Why are employees the most valuable intangible assts? Retrieved July 12, 2021, from https://www.educba.com/employee-most-valuable-intangible-assets/

Sienkiewicz, A. (2020) What Is a Chatbot? 11 Benefits of Chatbots That Will Help Your Business Grow. Retrieved February 9, 202 from https://www.tidio.com/blog/what-is-a-chatbot/?utm_source=google&utm_medium=cpc&utm_campaign=blogpost&utm_content=what_is_a_chatbot&utm_term=chatbots%20meaning&gclid=CjwKCAiA-P7xBRAvEiwAow-VaYmwA6t904BrIBfs2b62sbvYUApog9gpChdWk7-tXFvA6wfgArtjbhoCPuEQAvD_BwE

Silverthorne, S. (1992). Wang Laboratories Failed to Listen to Its Customers. The Peninsula Times Tribune. August 30, 1992.

Simonite, T., (2019) Robots Will Take Jobs From Men, the Young, and Minorities. Retrieved on May 10, 2021 from https://www.wired.com/story/robots-will-take-jobs-from-men-young-minorities/

Simonite, T. (2021) Don't End Up on This Artificial Intelligence Hall of Shame. Retrieved on February 2, 24, 2021 from https://www.wired.com/story/artificial-intelligence-hall-shame/?bxid=5cec28123f92a45b30f3bf54&cndid=4976163&esrc=Wired_etl_load&mbid=mbid%3DCRMWIR012019%0A%0A&source=EDT_WIR_%E2%80%A6

Simonite, T. (2021) Now That Machines Can Learn, Can They Unlearn?. Retrieved on February 24, 2022 from https://www.wired.com/story/machines-can-learn-can-they-unlearn/?bxid=5cec28123f92a45b30f3bf54&cndid=4976163&esrc=Wired_etl_load&source=EDT_WIR_NEWSLETTER_0_TRANSPORTATION_ZZ&utm_brand=wired&utm_campaign=aud-dev&utm_mailing=WIR_Daily_081921_FastForward&utm_medium=email&utm_source=nl&utm_term=WIR_TopClickers_EXCLUDE_Transportation

Simonite, T. (2021) The Exile. Wired July/August. 115-127.

Singh, A. (2006). International business Machines (IBM). Failure of Large Computer Companies. P. 19

Sloan, A. and Anderson, L. (2108) Adaptive learning unplugged: Why instructors matter more than ever. Retrieved January 14, 2020 from https://er.educause.edu/articles/2018/6/adaptive-learning-unplugged-why-instructors-matter-more-than-ever

Smith, E. (2017) The Great Failure of Wang Laboratories, the David to IBM's Goliath. Retrieved October 1, 2019 from https://www.vice.com/en_us/article/vvxby3/the-great-failure-of-wang-laboratories-the-david-to-ibms-goliath

Soininvaara, O. (2019) AI and human obsolescence – what you should know. Retrieved February 24, 2020 from https://www.solita.fi/en/blogs/ai-and-human-obsolescence-what-you-should-know/

Soltan, H. & Mostafa, S. (2015) Lean and agile performance framework for manufacturing enterprises. Procedure Manufacturing 2, p. 476-484. Science Direct.

Soper, S. (2021) Fired by Bot at Amazon: 'It's You Against the Machine'; Contract drivers say algorithms terminate them by email – even when they have done nothing wrong. Retrieved on February 24, 2021 from https://www.bloomberg.com/news/features/2021-06-28/fired-by-bot-amazon-turns-to-machine-managers-and-workers-are-losing-out

Strada Education Network (2019) Institute for the Future of Work. Innovation in Work & Learning. Retrieved on December 10, 2019 from https://stradaeducation.org/innovation-in-work-learning/.

Sumser, J. (2018) *This Chatbot Developer is Disrupting the R&D Process*. San Francisco: Human Resource Executive.

Surowiecki, J. (2017) Robots Won't Take All Our Jobs. Retrieved on May 5, 2021 from http://wired.com/2017/08/robots-will-not-take-your-job/

Sutter, J. (2018). *Is AI necessary for effective data clean-ups?* Innovation Enterprise Channels.

The Year When AI Will Humanize the Workplace. Oracle Human Capital Management. Retrieved from https://blogs.oracle.com/2018%3a-the-year-when-ai-will-humanize-the-workplace on August 29, 2019.

Tapscott, D. and Tapscott, A. (2017) *The Blockchain Revolution and Higher Education*. March/ April 2017. Educause.

Thibodeau, P. (2018). HR automation tops 2019's six big trends. Tech Target Network.

Thomson Reuters (2020) Demystifying Artificial Intelligence. A legal guide through the noise. Retrieved on February 24, 2020 from https://legal.thomsonreuters.com/en/insights/white-papers/demystifying-ai

Topol, E. (2019) Deep Medicine: How Artificial Intelligence Can Make Healthcare Human Again. Basic Books.

Tulinayo, F. Ssentume, P. and Najjuma, R. (2018) Digital technologies in resource constrained higher institutions of learning: a study on students' acceptance and usability. Springer Open. Creative Commons.

Vasil, J. (2006). Comparison. Failure of Large Computer Companies. P. 38-40.

Wang, R. (2018). Intelligent Workforce Automation Helps Organizations Become More Productive and Agile. Redwood City: Oracle Corporation.

Waring, I. (2014) Why Did Digital Equipment Fail Retrieved October1, 2019 from https://www.ianwaring.com/2014/06/19/why-did-digital-equipment-corporation-fail/

Wasserman, T. (2019). 10 technologies that could change retail forever. http://cmo.adobe.com/articles/2017/10/10-technologies-helping-to-oerhaul-the-retail-expereience.html#gs.xe4vfg

Welsh, A. (2018) Health experts say parents need to drastically cut kids' screen time. Retrieved December 09, 2019 from https://www.cbsnews.com/news/parents-need-to-drastically-cut-kids-screen-time-devices-american-heart-association/.

West, S. M., Whittaker, M. and Crawford, K. (2019). Discriminating Systems: Gender, Race, and Power in AI. Creative Commons licensed 4.0.

Wisskirchen, G., Biacabe, B., Bormann, U., Muntz, A., Niehaus, G., Soler, G.J., von Brauchitsch, B. (2017). Artificial Intelligence and Robotics and Their Impact on the Workplace. IBA Global.

Wylie, I.R. (2016). Evolution and Revolution in Artificial Intelligence in Education. International Journal of Artificial Intelligence Education, p.582-599.

Yu Lian Qui and Guo Fang Xia (2020) Research on Cost management Optimization of Financial Sharing Center Based RPA. Science Direct. Procedia Computer Science 166. 115-119.

Glossary of Acronyms

AI Artificial Intelligence
AIED Artificial Intelligence in Education
AOCE Apple Open Collaborative Environment
API Application Program Interface
AR Augmented Reality
AWS Amazon Web Services

BIPA Biometric Information Privacy Act
BPO Business Process Outsourcing

CED Common Education Data Standards
CEO Chief Executive Officer
CEU Continuing Education Unit
CFO Chief Financial Officer
CMU Carnegie Mellon University
CRM Customer Relationship Management

DARPA Defense Advanced Research Projects Agency
DCC Digital Credentials Consortium
DEC Digital Equipment Corporation
DevOps Development and Operations
DG Data General
DOE Department of Education
DTL Distributed Ledger Technology

EBI Education Blockchain Initiative

ERP Enterprise Resource Planning

FERPA Family Educational Rights and Privacy Act
FTC Federal Trade Commission

GAN Generative Adversarial Network
GDP Gross Domestic Product
GDPR General Data Protection Regulation
GED (exam) General Education Development or Diploma
GUI Graphical User Interface

HP Hewlett-Packard
HR Human Resources
HRIS Human Resources Information Systems

IAT Intelligent Adaptive Tutors
IDC Individual Distributed Cognition
ILEs Interactive Learning Environments
IOT Internet of Things
IP Intellectual Property
IPA Intelligent Process Automation
IT Information Technology
ITS Intelligent Tutoring Systems

JIT Just in Time

KISS Knowledge Intensive Service Support

L&D Learning and Development
LMS Learning Management System
LRS Learning Record Store
LXP Learning Experience Platform

MAS Multiagent Systems
MIT Massachusetts Institute of Technology
ML Machine Learning
MOOCs Massive Online Open Courses
MySQL System Quarry Language

NLP Natural Language Processing

OCR Optical Character Recognition

PC Personal Computer
PEU Professional Education Unit
PoW Point of Work
PP&E Property, Plant and Equipment
PWC Price Waterhouse Cooper

QA Quality Assurance
QC Quality Control

ROI Return On Investment
RPA Robotic Process Automation

SDC System Distributed Cognition

SSI Self-sovereign Identity

STARA Smart Technology, Artificial intelligence, Robots and Algorithms

STEM Science, Technology, Engineering and Math

TQM Time Quality Management

UD Universal Design

VA Virtual Assistants

VC Verifiable credential

VR Virtual Reality

Index

Adaptive Learning (AL) 134, 135, 256

Adaptive Tutors (AT) 124, 201, 262

Agents 24, 27, 48, 98, 99, 100, 118, 136, 206, 221, 223

Agile 4, 13, 17, 18, 19, 21, 22, 24, 25, 26, 27, 28, 29, 31, 32, 40, 45, 46, 48, 50, 56, 58, 59, 60, 61, 63, 77, 79, 83, 84, 85, 107, 108, 109, 110, 111, 112, 113, 114, 115, 116, 117, 118, 119, 120, 121, 129, 137, 139, 147, 154, 205, 206, 230, 238, 239, 244, 248, 250, 251, 257, 259

Agile Manifesto 107

Agile Transformation 109, 110, 111, 113, 114, 116, 117

Agile Workplace 21, 22, 129, 137, 147, 205, 238

Agility 24, 26, 41, 43, 48, 63, 65, 66, 69, 85, 86, 100, 114

AI Incident Database 214

Alexa 1, 5, 42, 91, 100, 192, 202, 203, 204, 213, 216, 222

Algorithm 3, 4, 15, 30, 33, 42, 51, 77, 85, 91, 93, 96, 101, 124, 136, 146, 157, 170, 171, 176, 178, 183, 184, 189, 191, 192, 193, 195, 198, 208, 211, 212, 213, 217, 221, 224, 225, 228, 234, 250, 251, 257

Amazon 2, 5, 10, 38, 56, 65, 66, 67, 91, 126, 176, 178, 188, 192, 198, 203, 204, 208, 209, 210, 211, 222, 250, 257, 261

Amazon Echo 38

Amazon Web Services (AWS) 126, 178, 261

Android 203, 204

Apple 2, 56, 57, 59, 60, 62, 63, 64, 182, 203, 204, 225, 254, 261

Application Program Interfaces (API) 158, 161, 163, 261

Artificial Intelligence i, 7, 34, 41, 123, 131, 196, 237, 238, 239, 241, 242, 243, 245, 246, 247, 250, 251, 255, 256, 258, 259, 261, 263

Artificial Intelligence in Education (AIEd) 34, 123, 124, 131, 132, 134, 137, 139, 140

AT&T 201

Audit 3, 85, 97, 110, 161, 166, 183, 192, 194

Augmentation 16, 17

Augmented Reality (AR) 85, 136, 261

Authentication 143, 145

Automation 4, 16, 17, 21, 22, 38, 41, 48, 49, 67, 74, 75, 76, 77, 80, 87, 90, 93, 138, 148, 157, 158, 159, 161, 162, 163, 164, 165, 167, 168, 169, 170, 221, 227, 239, 240, 242, 245, 247, 248, 258, 259, 262, 263

Bias 3, 15, 30, 81, 85, 184, 187, 188, 189, 190, 191, 192, 193, 194, 195, 197, 198, 199, 217, 225, 228, 250

Biased Stereotypes 199

Big Data 1, 5, 21, 41, 44, 55, 99, 132, 176, 232

Black Box 71, 148, 191, 196, 212, 213
Blockchain 84, 141, 142, 143, 144, 145, 146, 147, 148, 149, 150, 151, 152, 153, 154, 155, 156, 247, 249, 252, 253, 258, 261
Bluetooth Beacons 202
Business Process Outsourcing (BPO) 160, 163, 261
Carnegie hour 128, 154
Certification 143
Chatbots 90, 91, 133, 205, 225, 252, 255
China 14, 42, 43, 44, 55, 56, 101, 202, 207, 215, 217, 226, 247, 250
Clearview 201, 202
Cloud 63, 203
Cognition 10, 26, 27, 28, 124, 138, 169, 224, 243, 252, 262, 263
Cognitive science 224
Cognitive System 26, 224
Cognizant 84, 85, 240
Collective Cognition 26
Collectively distributed cognition 26
Common Education Data Standards (CEDS) 151
Continuous Improvement 25, 31, 110, 111
Cortana 202, 204
COVID 94, 102, 145, 206, 227, 234
Credentials 141, 143, 144, 146, 147, 148, 149, 150, 151, 153, 162, 261
Cryptograph 141, 149
Customer Capital 181

Customer Relationship Management (CRM) 12, 261
Cybercrime 12, 85
Cybersecurity 84
Data General (DG) 57, 59, 61, 62, 63, 241, 245, 254, 261
Deep Learning 1, 5, 14, 17, 45, 51, 108, 171
Defense Advanced Research Projects Agency (DARPA) 2, 261
Delphi 225
Department of Education (DOE) 127, 148, 252, 253, 261
Deployment 3, 9, 42, 43, 131
Development and Operations (DevOps) 44, 112, 251, 261
Digital Capital 176, 177, 178, 239
Digital Credentials Consortium (DCC) 151, 261
Digital Equipment Corporation (DEC) 57, 58, 59, 61, 62, 243, 248, 261
Digitization 13, 184
Displacement 2, 3, 5, 9, 41, 86
Disruption 1, 5, 10, 14, 41, 42, 45, 46, 47, 48, 49, 51, 52, 53, 56, 57, 60, 68, 72, 79, 83, 90, 177
Distributed Cognition 26, 27, 224, 252, 262, 263
Distributed Ledger Technology (DTL) 141, 261
Duality 2, 8
Education 3, 4, 13, 15, 16, 17, 18, 25, 32, 34, 35, 36, 37, 41, 46, 47, 56, 57, 61, 77, 83, 86, 89, 93, 96,

101, 123, 125, 126, 127, 128, 129, 130, 131, 132, 135, 137, 138, 140, 141, 142, 143, 144, 145, 147, 148, 149, 150, 151, 152, 153, 154, 156, 180, 199, 227, 231, 233, 237, 238, 241, 247, 248, 249, 251, 252, 253, 257, 258, 259, 261, 262, 263, 272

Educational Data Mining (EDM) 123

Education Blockchain Initiative (EBI) 148, 261

Education System 32, 41, 125, 126

Email ii

Employment 21, 22, 34, 55, 67, 77, 90, 95, 138, 143, 144, 148, 149, 156, 197, 201, 232, 245, 247

Enterprise Resource Planning (ERP) 12, 79, 261

Expectations 12, 25, 83, 92, 101, 111, 126, 131, 134

Facebook 15, 76, 188, 193, 196, 198, 201, 202, 204, 224

Family Education Rights and Privacy Act (FERPA) 146, 147, 151, 262

Federal Trade Commission (FTC) 225, 262

Fourth Amendment 201

Freelance 94, 95

Future of Work 18, 47, 85, 187, 244, 254, 257

Gebru, Timnit 187

Gender Bias 191, 250

General Data Protection Act (GDPR) 14, 151, 262

General Education Development or Diploma (GED) 125, 262

General Intelligence 82

Gig Economy 182

Gig Workers 94, 95

Google 1, 2, 3, 5, 15, 30, 38, 55, 73, 76, 91, 96, 126, 138, 153, 176, 187, 188, 191, 193, 198, 201, 203, 204, 214, 225, 238

Google Home 38, 91

Gross Domestic Product (GDP) 75, 175, 177, 262

Healthcare 13, 22, 24, 28, 57, 59, 77, 81, 83, 85, 91, 96, 133, 182, 199, 231, 233, 258

Higher Education 123, 127, 128, 129, 130, 145, 150, 153, 154, 227, 231, 237, 258

Human Capital 150, 176, 180, 181, 242, 258

Human Interactions 23, 108, 215, 231

Human Needs 72, 235

Human Performance 1, 104

Human Resources (HR) 3, 10, 14, 90, 91, 92, 93, 94, 95, 104, 107, 108, 113, 123, 145, 149, 163, 169, 180, 185, 192, 196, 205, 206, 211, 227, 228, 233, 242, 245, 258, 262

IBM 2, 7, 55, 56, 57, 58, 60, 62, 63, 64, 159, 161, 207, 245, 256, 257

Individual Distributed Cognition (IDC) 224, 262

Instagram 201

Intangible Assets 175, 176, 177, 178, 179, 180, 182, 183, 184, 185, 186, 237, 238, 252, 254

Integration 17, 35, 97, 98, 110, 119, 158, 161, 170, 173, 182, 218, 228

Intellectual Capital 178, 181

Intelligent Adaptive Tutors (IAT) 124, 262

Intelligent Agents 24, 98, 99, 118

Intelligent Process Automation (IPA) 157, 168, 170, 171, 172, 248, 262

Intelligent Tutoring Systems (ITS) 124, 132, 262

Intelligent Tutor Systems (ITS) 124, 132, 262

Interaction 6, 23, 24, 32, 35, 99, 100, 107, 108, 124, 130, 134, 135, 137, 142, 169, 170, 206, 215, 216, 231

Interactive Learning Environments (ILE) 47, 262

International Business Machines (IBM) 2, 7, 55, 56, 57, 58, 60, 62, 63, 64, 159, 161, 207, 245, 256, 257

Internet of Things (IOT) 21, 33, 38, 44, 104, 130, 169, 216, 217, 262

iOS 203

Job Churn 74

Just in Time (JIT) 25, 35, 117, 131, 139, 262

K-12 86, 123, 125, 126, 127, 150, 156, 241

Knowledge Intensive Service Support (KISS) 27, 262

Kodak 66, 69, 79

Learning and Development (L&D) 1, 18, 31, 34, 47, 93, 95, 104, 129, 130, 180, 205, 262

Learning Management Systems (LMS) 128, 134, 228, 229, 262

Learning Record Store (LRS) 229, 263

Lifelong Learning 35, 36, 93, 111, 147, 148, 149, 152, 231

LinkedIn 201, 272

Little Data 1, 5, 44

Machine Learning (ML) 1, 5, 6, 7, 11, 17, 45, 51, 75, 80, 81, 82, 96, 98, 99, 118, 131, 157, 161, 164, 169, 170, 171, 183, 195, 224, 226, 227, 231, 263

Mann, Horace 125

Massachusetts Institute of Technology (MIT) 2, 7, 73, 127, 134, 151, 213, 241, 246, 254, 263

Massachusetts Miracle 62

Massive Online Open Courses (MOOC) 144, 263

McDonald's 5, 56, 207, 249

Meta 2

Microsoft 2, 60, 63, 64, 188, 193, 204, 217, 218, 225, 226

Minicomputers 60, 61, 62

Motorola 62

Multiagent Systems (MAS) 118, 263

MySQL 62, 263

National Center for Education Statistics (NCES) 151

Natural Language 7, 44, 78, 91, 98, 99, 124, 131, 157, 170, 223, 263

Natural Language Processing (NLP) 170, 223, 263

Neural Networks 6, 124, 136, 187, 226

O'Brien, Tim 217, 218

Obsolescence 41, 42, 47, 48, 49, 51, 52, 53, 56, 57, 60, 68, 73, 81, 237, 257

Optical Character Recognition (OCR) 100, 263

Organizational Capital 180, 181

Pepper 74

Personal Assistants 133

Property, Plant and Equipment (PPE) 175, 177, 263

Quality Assurance (QA) 160, 263

Quality Control (QC) 160, 263

Redundancy 3, 14, 24, 28

Regression to the Mean 189, 190, 195

Research Triangle 61

Retail 22, 33, 52, 56, 57, 65, 66, 67, 68, 72, 89, 159, 178, 182, 233, 247, 249, 259

Robot 1, 10, 11, 13, 14, 15, 17, 33, 41, 50, 56, 67, 68, 73, 74, 75, 77, 79, 87, 98, 102, 103, 105, 168, 215, 221, 222, 240, 242, 243, 244, 249, 252, 255, 258, 263

Robotic Process Automation (RPA) 90, 91, 93, 97, 98, 99, 157, 158, 159, 160, 161, 162, 163, 164, 165, 166, 167, 168, 169, 170, 171, 172, 173, 178, 206, 239, 242, 244, 247, 253, 259, 263

Robot Ready 18, 254

Russia 202

Science, Technology, Engineering and Math (STEM) 76, 264

Segment Retreat 79

Self-Driving 75, 216

Self-Sovereign Identity (SSI) 145, 146, 147, 263

Siri 1, 192, 202, 204

Smart Machines 6, 123

Smart Technology, Artificial intelligence, Robots and Algorithms (STARA) 33, 34, 239, 263

Smart Technology, Artificial Intelligence, Robots, and Algorithms (STARA) 33, 34, 239, 263

Smith, Adam 180

Specific Intelligence 82

Systematic Bias 30

System Distributed Cognition (SDC) 224, 263

The Wealth of Nations 180

Tik-Tok 201

Total Quality Management (TQM) 25, 117, 264

Transparency 3, 50, 114, 117, 141, 143, 144, 145, 146, 147, 191, 192, 194, 197, 198, 207, 212, 217

Twitter 201, 215

Unemployment 33, 41, 44, 70, 74, 80, 88, 233

Universal Design (UD) 136, 137, 264

Upskilling 94, 115, 234

Upwork 148

Venmo 201

Verifiable credentials (VC) 151, 264

Virtual Assistants (VA) 47, 264

Virtual Reality (VR) 37, 47, 85, 135, 136, 214, 264

Voice Technology 37

Wang Laboratories 36, 57, 59, 60, 61, 62, 243, 247, 254, 255, 257, 259

Watson 56, 64, 207, 232

YouTube 201, 214

Zip Recruiter 148

Bobbe Baggio, Ph.D.

Since 2002, Bobbe Baggio has been CEO of Advantage Learning Technologies, Inc. a company that provides programs, products and research for workplace learning. She believes that technologies are here to help everyone and to enhance human performance. Her area of expertise is the integration of technologies to enhance human performance including adult and workplace learning. She was Associate Provost of the School of Adult and Graduate Education (SAGE) at Cedar Crest College in Allentown, PA. She was the Associate Dean of Graduate Programs and Online Learning at American University in Washington, D.C. and was previously Program Director of the MS program in Instructional Technology Management at La Salle University in Philadelphia, PA. Her background includes IT Director, Director of Management Consulting and Senior Scientist.

Bobbe is the author of seven books, an engaging public speaker, strategic advisor and educator in the field of instructional technologies and learning. She was a consultant in learning and talent development for a global and virtually connected workforce. Her expertise draws upon her experience as a Fortune 100 IT manager, 20 years of consulting experience, and her doctoral studies in instructional design for online learning. Examples of clients include The Federal Reserve Bank, Pfizer, Novartis, Johnson & Johnson, University of Pennsylvania, DOD, PASSHE, Merck, BMS, KPMG, Siemens, Ticketmaster, IMG, Tyco Engineering, Fisher, Christiana Care Health System, Cisco, Ralph Lauren, Liz Clayborn and Adobe and others.

Her books Include:

The Visual Connection
The Pajama Effect
Virtual Touchpoints
#WFH
AI@Work
Analyzing Digital Discourse and Human Behavior in Modern Virtual Environments, Ed.
Anonymity and Learning in Digitally Mediated Communication: Trust and Authenticity in Cyber Education

LinkedIn Profile: https://www.linkedin.com/in/bobbe-baggio-ph-d-3561769/

Website: https://a-l-t.com/

www.ingramcontent.com/pod-product-compliance
Lightning Source LLC
Chambersburg PA
CBHW070731020526
44118CB00035B/1165